Liberal Peacebuilding and the Locus of Legitimacy

Liberal peacebuilding too often builds neither peace nor Liberalism. In a growing number of cases, people aren't rejecting and relegating democracy because it's bad; they're challenging it because it isn't relevant to their priorities and needs. The peacebuilding 'moment' — when consent for intervention is present and the opportunity to build a sustainable social contract between peacebuilders and people is most fruitful — is being squandered. This relationship, between governed and governance, relies on mutual needs realization, but there is no formal or informal requirement and mechanism for ascertaining what the 'subjects' of peacebuilding might prioritize. Instead, peacebuilders give the 'subjects' of peacebuilding what they think they should have.

This legitimacy gap — between what peacebuilders give and what subjects want — is the subject of this book. Through a range of empirical case studies conducted by country specialists, the book reveals that, when asked, people often prioritize roads, electricity, jobs, housing, schooling and pertinent justice (amongst other things) in the immediate aftermath of war. We find that mapping this locus of legitimacy may help develop the kind of relationship upon which the sustainability of any social contract between governed and governance rests.

This book was originally published as a special issue of the *Journal of Intervention and Statebuilding*.

David Roberts is Senior Lecturer in International Relations at Loughborough University, UK. He is the author of four books on positive peace and numerous articles on peacebuilding, human security and Cambodia.

Liberal Peacebuilding and the Locus of Legitimacy

Edited by
David Roberts

LONDON AND NEW YORK

First published 2015
by Routledge

2 Park Square, Milton Park, Abingdon, Oxfordshire OX14 4RN
711 Third Avenue, New York, NY 10017

Routledge is an imprint of the Taylor & Francis Group, an informa business

First issued in paperback 2018

Copyright © 2015 Taylor & Francis

All rights reserved. No part of this book may be reprinted or reproduced or utilised in any form or by any electronic, mechanical, or other means, now known or hereafter invented, including photocopying and recording, or in any information storage or retrieval system, without permission in writing from the publishers.

Notice:
Product or corporate names may be trademarks or registered trademarks, and are used only for identification and explanation without intent to infringe.

British Library Cataloguing in Publication Data
A catalogue record for this book is available from the British Library

ISBN 13: 978-1-138-80135-6 (hbk)
ISBN 13: 978-1-138-37941-1 (pbk)

Typeset in Trebuchet MS
by RefineCatch Limited, Bungay, Suffolk

Publisher's Note
The publisher accepts responsibility for any inconsistencies that may have arisen during the conversion of this book from journal articles to book chapters, namely the possible inclusion of journal terminology.

Disclaimer
Every effort has been made to contact copyright holders for their permission to reprint material in this book. The publishers would be grateful to hear from any copyright holder who is not here acknowledged and will undertake to rectify any errors or omissions in future editions of this book.

Contents

Citation Information — vii

1. Everyday Legitimacy and Postconflict States: Introduction — 1
   David Roberts

2. Everyday Legitimacy in Post-Conflict Spaces: The Creation of Social Legitimacy in Bosnia-Herzegovina's Cultural Arenas — 11
   Stefanie Kappler

3. Health, Conflict, Stability and Statebuilding: A House Built on Sand? — 29
   Stuart Gordon

4. An Empirical Approach to Post-conflict Legitimacy: Victims' Needs and the Everyday — 45
   Simon Robins

5. Surveying South Sudan: The Liberal, the Local and the Legitimate — 65
   David Roberts

6. Everyday Legitimacy and International Administration: Global Governance and Local Legitimacy in Kosovo — 87
   Nicolas Lemay-Hébert

Index — 105

Citation Information

The chapters in this book were originally published in the *Journal of Intervention and Statebuilding*, volume 7, issue 1 (March 2013). When citing this material, please use the original page numbering for each article, as follows:

Chapter 1
Everyday Legitimacy and Postconflict States: Introduction
David Roberts
Journal of Intervention and Statebuilding, volume 7, issue 1 (March 2013) pp. 1–10

Chapter 2
Everyday Legitimacy in Post-Conflict Spaces: The Creation of Social Legitimacy in Bosnia-Herzegovina's Cultural Arenas
Stefanie Kappler
Journal of Intervention and Statebuilding, volume 7, issue 1 (March 2013) pp. 11–28

Chapter 3
Health, Conflict, Stability and Statebuilding: A House Built on Sand?
Stuart Gordon
Journal of Intervention and Statebuilding, volume 7, issue 1 (March 2013) pp. 29–44

Chapter 4
An Empirical Approach to Post-conflict Legitimacy: Victims' Needs and the Everyday
Simon Robins
Journal of Intervention and Statebuilding, volume 7, issue 1 (March 2013) pp. 45–64

Chapter 5
Surveying South Sudan: The Liberal, the Local and the Legitimate
David Roberts
Journal of Intervention and Statebuilding, volume 7, issue 1 (March 2013) pp. 65–86

Chapter 6
Everyday Legitimacy and International Administration: Global Governance and Local Legitimacy in Kosovo
Nicolas Lemay-Hébert
Journal of Intervention and Statebuilding, volume 7, issue 1 (March 2013) pp. 87−104

Please direct any queries you may have about the citations to
clsuk.permissions@cengage.com

Everyday Legitimacy and Postconflict States: Introduction

David Roberts

Introduction

Stabilizing 'fragile', 'failed' and 'failing' states imagined to harbour or project malice and menace of some kind has attracted substantial academic attention and international intervention. Indeed, such matters are very much front and centre of policy and theory debates in the discipline of International Relations, where once such issues would have 'only' attracted the attention of 'lesser' subject areas like peace and conflict studies or development. Successful management of this security–development 'nexus', wherein the development of the alien Other along liberal lines is argued to render the purported security problem moot, is underpinned by and underpins the idea of the Liberal Peace, and the various international interventions such an ontology sanctions. Through this transformative force, the problematized alien nation is assimilated into the liberal international through conditioned adoption of Weberian state-centric institutions. Attempts to pacify and promote such spaces revolve around the duopoly of political and economic liberalization as the core objectives and methods of postconflict peacebuilding, which is audited and legitimated in concordance with the ideological priorities of global governance, which are fundamentally neoliberal (Call and Cousens 2008, Slotin et al. 2010). Thus, postconflict peacebuilding, wherein unstable polities are stabilized through democratization and capitalization (as distinct from postconflict development), is presently legitimated by according with external preferences and liberal norms.

The track record of this approach is unenviable, as even its supporters are beginning to concede (Paris 2010). Persistent political stability rarely ensues in the wake of the peacebuilders' departure, and Liberal democracy is rarely found beyond basic technical practices and local nomenclature, undermining both the real and rhetorical rationales for intervention. These conditions are confronted in orthodox circles with more technical managerialism of elite institutions and actors, and the relegation epistemologically and ontologically of the social base upon which the elites depend for their legitimacy. Theirs is not the only offer on the table, however.

Fourth generation, critical peacebuilding scholarship argues that the prevailing approach undermines prospects for generating the legitimacy that lies at the heart of a durable social contract between state and society, upon which sustainable peace depends (Reno 2008, Richmond 2008). Research is instead directed at processes that concord with internal preferences. The question of what priorities and institutions *would* generate local legitimacy and thence more relevant and sustainable relations and peace without being solely and implausibly indigenous, however, remain much underrepresented in the literature. The purpose of the research and discussion in this special issue is to identify the terms and conditions upon which postconflict societies might consent to be governed. It is not to be confused with establishing development agendas and priorities, although these may overlap. It concerns postconflict stabilization and the means by which reciprocating respect between state and society can create a stable political platform for peaceful development, from within, as opposed to perpetuating the assumption that Liberal peacebuilding will automatically generate such consent.

The Literature and Local Legitimacy

What does the literature say about local legitimacy? The prevailing approach to postconflict peacebuilding addresses and empowers elites and Weberian institutions whilst offering people the plebiscite. This approach rests on the assumption that 'people will accept a political authority because they have been given the right to take part in free and fair elections' (Lindberg 2006, p. 1). Its origins can also be found in the work of a variety of scholars like Guillermo O'Donnell (2007), Allen Buchanan (2002) and Bruce Gilley (2006), amongst others. Thus, from these perspectives, government and affiliated institutions are legitimate because people have been allowed to vote for them in elections; the act of acceptance confers the right to rule. Polling forms the centrepiece of postconflict peacebuilding, presented as consent for international ingress whilst simultaneously providing an egress point for peacebuilders. Elections legitimate the state and the wider peacebuilding project, carried out under the ideological aegis of liberalism.

This does not mean the orthodoxy does not consider legitimacy in more thoughtful ways, however. Charles Call has recently attempted to challenge the intellectual monoculture in liberalism that tends to paint all problems in the same light, thus enabling it to advance the same solution to those problems across the board in Sisyphean nature. He proposes to rethink 'failed' and 'failing' states conceptually because they represent crude generalizations and reductions that inhibit our capacity effectively to confront them. Instead, he advocates categorizing what must inevitably be, he suggests, widely varied conditions. Part of this reconceptualization is to posit a 'legitimacy gap', between what states are programmed to do and what people will support their states for doing. His framework for thinking about legitimacy remains orientated around the same assumptions regarding elections. He states that legitimacy can be judged to be absent or present depending on 'whether the regime's rules and/or processes are sufficiently transparent and accountable to permit popular free expression and participation' (Call 2011, p. 308). This is because they are the only 'objective' definitions of legitimacy available in such circumstances. Call rejects the idea of asking for people's opinions about what might make their government legitimate to them on the grounds that they might not feel free enough to answer openly, and that the subjectivity of social surveys renders them ineffective and thus undesirable. Despite the appearance of a substantial critique of existing convention, then, this work remains well within existing liberal ontological and epistemological boundaries. Indeed, some might say it goes further, because it simultaneously sanctions and obscures popular exclusion behind the rhetoric of liberal 'transparency' and 'participation'.

Other attempts have been made from within the liberal policy sector, as distinct from academia. For example, the influential International Peace Institute (IPI) claims to place 'the concept of legitimacy—as both a means to building state capacity and an end in itself—squarely at the centre of the debate' on unstable polities. It notes a 'common undercurrent' in terms of the 'vulnerability of the government to recurring crises of legitimacy and authority'. It goes on to comment that 'international actors generally have inadequate understanding of ... legitimacy' in such spaces (Slotin *et al.* 2010, p. 8). Yet, despite this statement, the remainder of the report discusses the tools available to foreigners for them to assess such matters, returning again to the position of validation from without, rather than from within. The IPI report perpetuates the epistemological assumptions derived from a paternalist ontology never far removed from imperialism (Roberts 2011). Reducing legitimacy to 'objective' terms that can be observed and measured is only an extension in thinking of the tendency to conflate global technical 'solutions' with local political 'problems' through holding elections that fail to confront the political economy of elite contestation for authority. The centrality of the local to the generation of legitimacy is peripheral to this IPI study, perpetuating patterns of exclusion of people, knowledge and politics in the orthodox scholarship and narrowing what may be considered politically legitimate in the eyes of the citizenry expected to sanction political authority in a democratizing society.

A More Critical Critique?

There is little new, then, under the orthodox sun. But a variety of scholars and institutions beyond the mainstream is examining the nature of political legitimacy in postconflict spaces from a different perspective. A key difference appears to concern the object of legitimacy and its political vector. Thus, for orthodoxists, the object is the global: it is the priorities of the international system that direct the form and content of legitimacy in its own image. The state mirrors global governance—rules, regimes and institutions in order to legitimate itself, and authority then comes from the top down. In the following literature, the object is more local: it is the anticipated priorities of the national that shape legitimacy in the image of local people's will. The state in this perspective mirrors local governance issues in order to self-sanction, and authority comes from below, from the bottom up. Thus, according to Bo Rothstein, for example (and suspending any Schumpeterian critique), the electoral moment is not enough to instaurate a durable bond between state and society. Instead, he argues, 'a government can achieve political legitimacy [if] it serves some notion of the common interest in coordinating citizens' activities in a socially beneficial way' (Rothstein 2009, p. 313). Rothstein proposes that the outcome of interactions between state and society is that both must benefit in some meaningful way in the periods between electoral moments for peaceable relations between the two to be sustained. In order for the state to benefit from social acquiescence to its presumed authority, after it has been elected it must offer and deliver something substantial to the citizenry that the population wants. The conclusion is compellingly different from the orthodoxy. Rothstein argues not that electoral democracy is in any way wrong. Rather, he maintains that his is an argument 'against the idea that it can serve as the main pillar of creating political legitimacy'. He adds that:

> Electoral democracy is highly overrated when it comes to creating legitimacy. On the contrary, legitimacy is created, maintained and destroyed not by the input but by the output side of the political system [and that] political legitimacy depends on the quality of government, not the quality of elections or political representation. (Rothstein 2009, p. 313; and see Kotzian 2010)

This is similar conceptually to Monika Francois and Inder Sud's (2006, p. 147) 'performance legitimacy'. They write that:

> Democratic legitimacy is based on social acceptance of the 'rules of the game'. Even if the outcome of the game—government performance—is suboptimal, it is tolerated because the processes by which it was achieved are agreed upon. In contrast, performance legitimacy is based on the outcome of the game: fulfillment of state functions. (Francois and Sud 2006, p. 147)

They add that while the process of constitutional liberalization and democratization may proffer some legitimacy in the eyes of society, 'even democratic politics is unlikely to save a state that cannot deliver on its basic responsibilities: physical protection of its citizens and improvements in their living standards' in the wider context of rising expectations (Francois and Sud 2006, p. 148). This leaves us, however, swinging to the other sweep of the pendulum. Is there a position in between? Merilee Grindle (2007) argues that there is. She suggests that a compromise between democratic and performance legitimacy might be 'good enough' governance. From this perspective, legitimacy might be understood:

> In relation to people's material and symbolic expectations and perceptions. Lack of or poor legitimacy is thus a major contributor to state fragility. It deprives the state of peoples' support; it prohibits the making of a political community or identity, and prevents the state from acting efficiently at the lowest possible social and financial costs. Emphasizing that legitimacy has to do with peoples' beliefs and perceptions and daily social practices of the state allows us to look into the various sources that a state, and other institutions, may draw upon to shore up legitimacy. (Bellina et al. 2009, p. 8)

In other words, there is a literature moving away from making state behaviour relevant first and mainly to neoliberal ideology and global governance benchmarks, towards making it relate to the needs of the people over whom the state claims jurisdiction. The two cannot be fully separated, of course, since the stability anticipated from local legitimacy also feeds the wider liberal interest in maintaining its own security. However, the institutional emphasis has relied on the rather naïve assumption that 'if we build them, people will come'. They have not, as the record to date shows.

An understanding that states must work for people in ways that they want—that they must be internally validated—is clearly crystallizing. For it to be meaningful, however, the literature must refine how it may appear in practice. With this demand in mind, Katia Papagianni (2008) has identified three internal dimensions to local legitimacy. These include ensuring the means through which elites may peacefully contest the right to rule, and the presence of effective mechanisms by which the public may anoint authority on one or a combination of these elites. To this, she adds the need to maintain public order. To varying degrees, orthodox peacebuilding presently accommodates such provision by supporting the electoral process as a means to both ends. The same may be said of public order, managed through Security Sector Reform (SSR) which entails the retraining and restraining of domestic security forces and constabulary along liberal lines. These, however, attract more technical interventions which alone cannot adequately address underlying political dilemmas such as local perceptions of authority that are not grounded in liberal traditions. Nor do they address the absence of basic needs common to citizens and constabulary alike that contribute to 'illiberal' behaviours amongst the constabulary and the armed forces. Because of this lacuna, Papagianni identifies other areas that are not treated in orthodox peacebuilding but which also legitimate the state to a population. She argues that statebuilding 'is most likely to generate legitimacy for the state when it is inclusive of all major political forces and open to the participation of the public but also places a priority on maintaining public order *and delivering services*' (Papagianni 2008, p. 50; emphasis added). This challenges not the basis of liberalism but the prevailing priorities that liberal peacebuilding invokes in postconflict spaces. It suggests we reconsider not the underlying idea necessarily, but instead address the orthodox preoccupation with balloting and its tendency to exclude complex social dynamics of legitimation. This is not least because the relationships and processes involved in wider public provision not only derive from a radically different ontology and ideology of state, but are also normally poorly understood and tolerated by international peacebuilders.

Jennifer Milliken and Keith Krause also point to the satisfaction, at least in part and in theory, of people's everyday needs as a source of legitimacy for the state (as opposed to providing for other rationales like human rights or basic needs regimes). They ask: 'what are the minimal conditions of governance required [for stable development]; and what are the roles and influence of the international community in creating these conditions?' (Milliken and Krause 2002, p. 761). Their answer expands from the standard response of security and order to the remit of social welfare and basic needs. They describe 'welfare and entitlement' as a 'powerful glue that binds citizens to their state' (Milliken and Krause 2002, p. 760). In mature democracies, this has often formed part of the social contract between governors and governed, expanding the duties of state beyond the original role of 'providing security from civil disorder and war' (Milliken and Krause 2002, p. 758). It is the view of Milliken and Krause (2002, p. 761) that most postcolonial states are not able effectively to organize welfare and, where they do, it is unbalanced and unfair because it is directed through systems of patronage and clientelism that exist as much to 'play a central role in regime legitimation and maintenance' as to serve local people. Such states may also be unable to provide such matters because they are forbidden from so doing by conditional lending by major international institutions like the World Bank.

In a similar vein, Christopher Clapham (2003, p. 92) has also suggested dependency relations between social care and state legitimacy, and argues that 'mayhem can be reduced, if not in every case prevented, by well-crafted intervention designed not only to strengthen states, but to meet the human needs that must ultimately justify their existence'. Clarifying the kind of provision deemed to be necessary to bond state to society beyond the technical, Michael Cichon and Krzysztof Hagemejer (2007, p. 169) argue that state intervention in welfare, broadly defined but related to the idea of the government serving everyday needs and lives, would produce the 'societal cohesion that is needed for long term economic development' and which contributes to the creation of state–societal stability.

Thus, the IR silo in which the peacebuilding debate has become relocated is now balanced by a literature proposing a more nuanced examination of the extent to which peacebuilding needs to be legitimate in the eyes of those who proffer the process as well as those who experience its edict.

The Special Issue's Contribution

How do the articles in this special issue contribute to this shift? The literature is presently weighted towards legitimacy being derived through securing hegemonic ideology and elite institutions rather than everyday life and social necessity, with the latter underrepresented and undervalued, resulting in 'the real world' in a substantial lacuna in local legitimacy. But Stefanie Kappler suggests that, far from a vacuum of legitimacy following on from orthodox peacebuilding interventions, local legitimacy is being engineered through the necessities and practices of everyday life. However, it may not be the state that is being legitimated. Kappler uses the example of Bosnia-Herzegovina to show that although international peacebuilding has failed to legitimate the formal, public arena of the state-institutional system it privileges, people have transferred the source of mass legitimacy and respect to what she terms the 'semi-public' arena, or 'local cultural spaces'. The common interests of everyday life have propelled practices that resonate with a broader cross-section of everyday life, cementing public trust to cultural and social bodies that earn it by their relevance to people's needs. This process has created an alternative social legitimacy that revolves around institutions and norms that have been substituted by people in the absence of their provision from central sources of state advanced in orthodox approaches. Thus, to some degree, the case of Bosnia-Herzegovina suggests that although legitimacy is not routinely directed to the institutions privileged as a matter of course in the neoliberal model of peacebuilding, it is in fact alive and well, but directed towards cultural and social bodies that have been created by people to fill the gap left by state-centric approaches. This mobility of legitimacy is widely borne out in other research that emphasizes the legitimacy of informal and hybrid formal–informal agencies in postconflict spaces (Roberts 2008, Mac Ginty 2010).

Thus, there is evidence that securing public needs is an important source of local legitimacy. In the limited literature that does attend to public need and local legitimacy, scholars like Susan Woodward (2002) have pointed to the health sector as a means of cementing society to the state, on the assumption that state-centric provision of a mass need at the most basic level will engender a relationship of trust and respect to develop into a social contract. Stuart Gordon, however, takes exception in this issue to this drift in the literature. He argues that the evidence to support such an assertion is too 'flimsy' and without adequate substantiation, and reviews the data accordingly. He concludes that as well as undermining health delivery by tying its provision to a broader meaning, the data does not suggest a correlation between state health care and social regard in the first instance, and that, accordingly, the literature is misguided to propose such an approach.

Gordon's conclusions regarding the empirical data on social provision and public trust are, however, challenged in the work of Simon Robins, who applies primary empirical data gathered in two recent field exercises in Nepal and Timor-Leste to the debate. Robins couches this data in a critique of fourth-generation peacebuilding literature which reflects Roland Paris' (2010) concerns regarding the conceptual vagueness and lack of any concrete imagining of what an 'emancipatory' approach might look like. Robins draws from qualitative interviews of local people to ascertain what peace would look like from a local perspective, were people to be asked what they favoured, rather than given what peacebuilding determines. His empirical study offers a qualitative representation of peacebuilding as defined by local people, with the aim of understanding their needs, priorities and vision of peacebuilding for their communities. It allows an understanding to emerge of how the 'conflict-affected' conceive of legitimacy and performance of government and governance, with victims emphasizing basic needs, the addressing of issues of marginalization, and the incorporation of indigenous understandings of the meaning of peace.

This internal dynamic reflects Stefanie Kappler's findings in Bosnia-Herzegovina, reinforcing the notion that although neoliberal peacebuilding may be hegemonic, it does not mean there is a tabula rasa in postconflict spaces, or that people do not have various degrees of agency and capacity and create institutions, liberal or 'illiberal', that earn their loyalty in the vacuum left by irrelevant or dysfunctional state priorities.

The emphasis on primary empirical data is continued in David Roberts' work, which builds on the need for alternative epistemes in the process of understanding what kind of peace is desired by people in postconflict spaces. It presents the findings of a locally-managed survey aimed at identifying what local people want the immediate postconflict space to look like. This data was compared with other literatures that have drawn the same epistemological conclusions and have deployed similar methodologies, within Southern Sudan and more broadly. It shows that whilst there was inevitable diversity of opinion and priorities across heterogeneous population groups, many people did not consider the matter of government, democracy or development in terms of legitimacy, but most people identified aspects of development before democracy, however it was understood. Perhaps most importantly, it points to the need to consider how the idea of legitimacy itself is deeply problematic, and requires further consideration before an effective methodology can be deployed.

Finally, Nicolas Lemay-Hébert considers questions of legitimacy in international administrations that are superimposed on societies and tasked with managing most aspects of government. Using Kosovo as his case study, Lemay-Hébert shows that the dominance of the international administration proved to be its downfall; in ignoring popular groundswells of opinion and desire, and acting in ways perceived as partisan, it undermined its own authority and thus legitimacy.

Summary

The mainstream literature persists in tying the achievement of state legitimacy to the provision of specific political institutions advancing particularist liberal values considered prime in contemporary Europe and the US. This is expected to deliver political stability and thence peace. In reality, however, centralized Weberian institutions have not generated social deference and loyalty because their priorities are divorced from those of a broad cross-section of society, which prefers often to favour local informal agencies that deliver basic needs, be they water, roads or security. This leaves a legitimacy lacuna, the matter of which is explored throughout this special issue of the *Journal of Intervention and Statebuilding*. It appears that, in contrast with mainstream expectations, pre-existing or new informal local bodies generate degrees of loyalty that their democratic counterparts do not because they are not focused on local needs. Postconflict states are 'illiberal' because liberalism is irrelevant to and unrepresentative of a majority in the early stages of peacebuilding. And it also appears that emergent legitimacy derives from varying provision of locally-determined basic needs by locally-originating (and sometimes externally-supported) informal institutions, rather than externally-imposed political agendas, in parallel with orthodox approaches, assured of their presence by the power of ideological hegemony.

Notes on Contributor

David Roberts is Senior Lecturer in Peace and Conflict Studies at the University of Ulster.

References

Bellina, S. et al., 2009. *The legitimacy of the state in fragile situations*. Norway: Norwegian Agency for Development Cooperation.
Buchanan, A., 2002. Political legitimacy and democracy. *Ethics*, 112, 689–719.
Call, C., 2011. Beyond the 'failed state': towards conceptual alternatives. *European journal of international relations*, 17 (2), 303–326.
Call, C. and Cousens, E., 2008. Ending wars and building peace: international responses to war-torn societies. *International studies perspectives*, 9, 1–21.
Cichon, M. and Hagermeyer, K., 2007. Changing the development policy paradigm: investing in a social security floor for all. *International social security review*, 60 (2–3), 169–196.
Clapham, C., 2003. The global–local politics of state decay. *In:* R. Rotberg, ed. *When states fail: causes and consequences*. Princeton, NJ: Princeton University Press.
Francois, M. and Sud, I., 2006. Promoting stability and development in fragile and failed states. *Development policy review*, 24 (2), 141–160.
Gilley, B., 2006. The determinants of state legitimacy: results for 72 countries. *International political science review*, 27 (1).
Grindle, M., 2007. Good enough governance revisited. *Development policy review*, 25 (5), 533–574.
Lindberg, S., 2006. *Democracy and elections in Africa*. Baltimore, MD: Johns Hopkins University.
Mac Ginty, R., 2010. Hybrid peace: the interaction between top-down and bottom-up peace. *Security dialogue*, 41 (4), 391–412.
Milliken, J. and Krause, K., 2002. State failure, state collapse, and state reconstruction: concepts, lessons and strategies. *Development and change*, 33 (2), 753–774.

O'Donnell, G., 2007. The perpetual crises of democracy. *Journal of democracy*, 18 (1), 5–9.

Papagianni, K., 2008. Participation and state legitimation. *In*: C. Call and V. Wyeth, eds. *Building states to build peace*. Boulder, CO: Lynne Rienner.

Paris, R., 2010. Saving liberal peacebuilding. *Review of international studies*, 36, 337–365.

Reno, W., 2008. Bottom-up statebuilding? *In*: C. Call and V. Wyeth, eds. *Building states to build peace*. Boulder, CO: Lynne Rienner.

Richmond, O., 2008. *Peace in international relations*. London: Routledge.

Roberts, D., 2008. Hybrid polities and indigenous pluralities: advanced lessons in statebuilding. *Journal of intervention and statebuilding*, 2 (1), 63–86.

Roberts, D., 2011. *Liberal peacebuilding and global governance: beyond the metropolis*. London: Routledge.

Rothstein, B., 2009. Creating political legitimacy: electoral democracy versus quality of government. *American behavioral scientist*, 53 (3), 311–330.

Slotin, J., Wyeth, V. and Romita, P., 2010. *Power, politics and change: how international actors assess local context*. New York: International Peace Institute.

Woodward, S., 2002. Economic priorities for successful peace implementation. *In*: S.J. Stedman, D. Rothchild and E. Cousens, eds. *Ending civil wars: the implementation of peace agreements*. Boulder: Lynne Rienner.

Everyday Legitimacy in Post-Conflict Spaces: The Creation of Social Legitimacy in Bosnia-Herzegovina's Cultural Arenas

Stefanie Kappler

The international community has long been criticized for its lack of social legitimacy in Bosnia-Herzegovina and its creation of a dysfunctional public space in the light of people's everyday experiences of peace. This article contends that, as a result, legitimacy has been moved from such public spaces to semi-public spaces, wherein the public and the private are interrelated. One example is local cultural arenas, where hopes emerging in people's everyday lives are projected onto alternative visions of peace and a corresponding social contract. In that sense, cultural agencies have served as alternative social locations of legitimacy due to their closer connection to people's lives and needs.

Introduction

A poll conducted in Bosnia-Herzegovina (BiH) in August 2010 presented the following results:

> An overwhelming majority feel that BiH is moving in the wrong direction. Almost nine-in-ten citizens (87%) say that things in BiH are moving in the wrong direction, a slightly higher percentage than observed in earlier waves of research conducted in October 2009 and April 2010. ...
>
> Only one citizen in 10 (12%) report that their lives have improved over the last 4 years. More than one half of citizens (54%) think that their lives have deteriorated; one-third say that their lives have not changed (34%). (National Democratic Institute 2010, p. 5)

Although stating a tendency of improvement, the United Nations Development Programme's (UNDP) Early Warning System 2010 Report confirms the overall dissatisfaction of the majority of Bosnians (51.8 per cent) with BiH's current political situation (UNDP 2010, p. 82).

These polls, although certainly not free from bias, reflect the extent to which people are unhappy with the current situation in BiH as well as with the political direction in which the country is moving. Empirical research suggests strongly this is because the formal political realm is dissociative; it does not resonate with everyday lives and fails to connect to people's needs and priorities. The elites and their internationally mandated institutions lack legitimacy in the eyes of ordinary folk; but what is this legitimacy, and in which spaces and around whom is it evolving?

This article builds on the example of the cultural arena to show how legitimacy has been re-configured in cultural spaces, including a private dimension of peace, representing microcosms of legitimacy and producing social contracts that are responsive to people's everyday experiences. Rolf Schwarz (2005, p. 441) reminds us that a social contract would need to (re-)establish a state–society relationship in terms of addressing questions of rights and representation. Based on this, the article suggests that a social contract would have to root these questions in people's everyday experiences of peace in order to make the latter sustainable and legitimate.

Previous research has raised the question of legitimacy and authority in different spheres. Roberto Belloni (2001) and Adam Fagan (2005) have outlined this problematique with respect to civil society actors, while Jonathan Fox (1999) has investigated religious legitimacy and its impacts on politics more generally. Against that background, this article focuses on the cultural arena as a sphere in which alternative structures of legitimacy are emerging. This is not to argue that the cultural sphere is representative of society or that it is superior to the spaces of civil society or religious actors. Nor does the article romanticize cultural activity in BiH. It aims to conceptualize the power of the cultural sphere to re-establish structures of legitimacy, albeit on a small scale. The following section provides a background to the formation of the formal public sphere in BiH through peacebuilding interventions and its associated lack of legitimacy.

Public Space and Formal Politics

'Public space' is an abstract notion of space, the idea of a platform of a political community, and is often considered the central sphere in which politics take place. In that sense, the public space of a society determines the extent to which people can participate in political processes and 'discuss and influence them through their interaction in the public sphere. The social codes and established norms in such a space then determine what is acceptable in that space according to the rules and norms established at a given point of time and context.

What may be of interest in the context of this paper is the double-edged meaning of public space, in its ability to empower and disempower the users of that space, or selected groups of users in that space. This is connected to Hannah Arendt's approach to the public realm, which she considers as an augmentation of human life in terms of its capacity to transcend the limits of what has long been considered 'private' by making interaction with other users of the public realm possible in the first place (Arendt 1958, 1967; see also Beacroft 2007). In that sense, the public realm represents a hybrid arena where the private and the political come together, which is the origin of political action and thus a basic necessity for the functioning of political life in a given context. Yet since this public space does not exist naturally, but is, according to Arendt (1958, 1967), an artificial creation of humans that needs to be constantly re-created to be kept alive, this realm is at the same time vulnerable to being co-opted by political actors, who may try to restrain its functions or, in the most extreme scenario, even abolish it and thus make political life dysfunctional in a society.

Michel Foucault (1980) expresses ambiguity towards the notion of space more generally, viewing it as a creation from structures of power and domination and thus raising concerns about disciplinary power within such spaces. On the other hand, in the Foucauldian sense, the presence of power hierarchies in a space implies the possibility of resistance, so, again, applying Foucault's ideas to the notion of a created public space, the latter can be considered empowering and disempowering at the same time. The concrete ways in which this plays out, as well as which actors are empowered and which are disempowered, depend on the context and the power relations within this space.

These dynamics are particularly relevant in an era in which the public/private division has been challenged (see, for instance, Horwitz 1982, Boyd 1997). In this context, Jeff Weintraub (1997) points to the differing meanings of 'private' vs. 'public' as well as the arbitrariness of boundary-drawing between the two categories. He suggests that the 'public' has often been viewed as the political and social world, while the 'private' has been understood to mean intimacy and family (Weintraub 1997, p. 2). However, public spheres are not necessarily completely detached from people's private identities. Rather, they represent spheres in which public and private identities merge and, as one might expect, become part of the political processes of that sphere. In that sense, people's private experiences of public affairs, such as the personal experience of conflict, development or human rights cannot be viewed as isolated from the ways in which they are dealt with publicly. The extent to which the state, for instance, empowers or disempowers certain sections of the population in turn feeds into how the state is experienced concretely in people's private lives and what its meanings in that context are. As a result, public space can serve as a space in which private and public identities are channelled into political processes, either to empower the users of the space, or, alternatively, to discipline them and limit their capacities of action when excluding their subjective experiences. The ways in which private processes can be translated into the public arena are dependent on their socio-historical context (Weintraub 1997, p. 37), the meaning of the distinction in this context as well as underlying interests and political strategies. The extent to which the private sphere of the users of the space can penetrate the public then determines who is empowered in the space in terms of accounting for the subjectivities in the private sphere. Against this background, one can ask what kind of political space has been created in the post-war peacebuilding context in Bosnia-Herzegovina. How much of it is connected to the democratic politics, rights and needs of its citizens, and how much of it is externally driven?

The public sphere in BiH is increasingly a divided space. This may have been the case in the past, but seems to be getting worse in the post-war context. This is a result of the two-entity structure as well as of ethnic divisions, with access to rights and benefits being organized along ethnic lines. This is not least due to the constitutional arrangement of the country, which results from the Dayton Peace Agreement (DPA) and its associated competitive practices, which ascribe rights in the political sphere and the possibility to participate in governing activities to a person's ethnic identity as Bosniak, Serb or Croat.[1] The fact that all 'constituent peoples' of BiH were granted a veto right in the DPA served as an encouragement for people to define their identities primarily as ethnic, before any other kind of identity. Sven Simonsen (2005) outlines how the institutionalization of ethnic identity can then undermine peacebuilding, while 'ethno-accentuation' may start to dominate other markers of identification.

In BiH, the state system created a deadlock for a future transformation of an ethnically divided public sphere, in terms of making change dependent on the agreement of all constituent nations of the country, which is a highly unlikely constellation. Interestingly enough, there is now a discourse within the Office of the High Representative (OHR), i.e. the principal organization supervising the implementation of the DPA and its associated blocking devices, which is asking the 'locals' to develop unblocking mechanisms and change the constant deadlock situation themselves. This seems like a somewhat ironic attitude, given that the OHR is responsible to ensure that the locals comply with the constitution included in the DPA, while the institution now asks for constitutional reform as well as the creation of local unblocking mechanisms despite the structural environment that is hostile to such changes. This represents a new development in the local ownership debate, which had in the past mostly been used as a tool to facilitate and legitimize external intervention. Yet it seems as if the debate is increasingly used to shift responsibility for the failures of intervention as well as the unresolved ethnic question. However, not only can we see ethnic divisions becoming engrained further (see Belloni 2004), but also a deepening of the gap between the two entities of the country.

Second, there is a tendency of the public space, not only in BiH, but of public space in general, to favour the elites of politics and the market. Indeed Morton Horwitz (1982, p. 1424) reminds us that generally the market serves as a legitimizing institution of the public sphere. Specifically referring to BiH, Michael Pugh (2002) shows how public space has become privatized, mainly by business elites who managed to instrumentalize post-war peacebuilding for their own benefits, drawing on clientelist networks to ensure their access to the 'spoils of peace'. In BiH, the EU is an interesting example of this, given that it is dependent on working with local political authorities to be able to apply its policies of conditionality as well as the European Partnership agenda. In that sense, the EU is giving additional power to political elites, thus indirectly impacting on the division of the public sphere. Timothy Donais (2003, p. 373) argues that the ambiguous and fragmented governing structures initially promoted by the international community have exacerbated issues of corruption, carving out spaces for local elites to co-opt the state system. This has been particularly evident in the party-ruled hydroelectric facilities in the Republika Srpska (RS) and Western Herzegovina as well as the Elektroprivreda Mostar, the profits of which were eventually channelled into party activities (Donais 2003, p. 370). There is in fact a growing acknowledgement within the international community that the policy of propping up the local political elites may cause a number of problems. In that context, it has been claimed that the OHR follows a strategy of 'feeding the hand that bites you' by putting money into big projects, which in turn ends up in the pockets of those who create new problems for the country.[2] Boris Divjak and Michael Pugh (2008) specifically remind us of the problems with criminality and corruption, politically and economically, so the public space is turning into a space of corruption, while the politics of the OHR have developed a rather high degree of tolerance towards issues of corruption. David Chandler (2002) has suggested that the policies of the OHR have failed to produce visible results with respect to corruption, partly as a result of its tendency to circumvent political institutions, treating them as the main problem rather than using them as vehicles for change.

Public space has become a space of elites, favouring specific actors: subjects as the ethnicized, the elites, the rich, have been empowered by the international peacebuilding community, while actors beyond those categories have been rendered powerless in public space. As a result, public space in post-war BiH has become de-personalized, de-politicized, shaped by structural constraints and divisions, while leaving little room for change and transgression of boundaries. At the same time, the public aims to exclude the private in order to work in the way its structures dictate.

(Il)Legitimacy in the Public Sphere

The consequences of public distance from the formal political sphere and the associated lack of legitimacy of the latter challenges the existing wisdom expressed by Katharina Coleman (2007) and others, who claim that the key locus of legitimacy is the international, not the local, and it is with that dissonance that this paper is concerned (see Franck 1990).

Generally, there seems to be an assumption that legitimacy is a feature of the public sphere, i.e. projected in the sphere that is accessible to all citizens and users of the public arena. Boutros Boutros-Ghali (1996, para. 18, 24), for instance, implies that democracy naturally creates legitimacy, pointing to the link between legitimacy and the political, and thus to its location in the public arena of voters and elections. In that sense, the idea of legitimacy has been linked to a notion of responsibility of the power-holders in front of the subjects of governance (Coicaud 2010, p. 18) as well as to its processual nature. In this context, Bruce Berman (2010, p. 136) suggests that legitimacy is in need of continuous re-creation, accounting for the constantly newly emerging configurations of a power regime.

Responding to these continuously changing configurations is a challenge for the institutions in power, particularly if we assume that legitimacy is a social construction, deriving from the different subjectivities of the subjects in a space. This relates to rights and needs—both material and psychological—as they constitute positions in a space. In this context, Anders Uhlin (2010, p. 22) reminds us that the creation of legitimacy always implies contested power struggles between highly diverse actors. Indeed, Ian Clark (2007, p. 254) suggests that legitimacy is a social property rather than the attribute of an action and must thus never be considered in isolation from its audience, where 'claims to legitimation are mediated through politics and consensus'. This audience in turn is situated in a political, economic, historical and cultural context, with legitimacy transcending the formal political sphere and extending into people's private lives and subjectivities.

Hence, if we are to re-situate legitimacy in the context of the everyday and its critical agencies, we need to take into account the associated complex negotiation processes. This involves questions, for instance, about which actors are considered capable of dealing with issues emerging in the daily lives of people, whether those be of a social, cultural, political or economic nature. It is therefore important to view the everyday as a space of agency in which subjectivities emerge and are used as tools of transformation, rather than as just containing banal repetitive actions (see Richmond 2011).

In BiH, this situation can be considered particularly eclectic and complex, with a variety of subjectivities coming together in the public sphere. There seems to be only little connection between the political authorities and those complex everyday experiences of people. Denisa Sarajlić-Maglić (2010) claims that the power-sharing mechanisms in the political system of BiH have allowed political elites to monopolize the political space, while at the same time subordinating the interests of other actors to their own interests in that space. She suggests that the international community has further engrained this system, which has resulted in an 'elite-packed democracy' and prevented autonomous actors from accessing the public sphere (Sarajlić-Maglić 2010, pp. 55, 56; see also Diamond 1999). This cannot be seen in isolation from the peacebuilding project in BiH, which has, whilst distorting the power constellations in the public sphere, depoliticized the liberal peace (Divjak and Pugh 2008, p. 373) in terms of removing its underlying social contract and transforming it into a technical operation, during the course of which 'peace' is measured by benchmarks and standards (see Kappler and Richmond 2011). Perhaps surprisingly, there is a clear realization of these problems, particularly within the OHR, which is much less engaged in the country nowadays, while at the same time not feeling able to leave before the respective reforms are implemented locally.[3] In agreement,

Chandler (2006a, p. 2) suggests that even ten years after Dayton, international actors have limited the autonomy of Bosnian representatives and removed the notion of 'political accountability for Bosnian citizens'. This represents a criticism of the practices of the High Representative, who is able to intervene in BiH's domestic policies without being democratically elected by the people. At the same time, this is also to challenge the approach of the EU for having accepted this 'highly restricted political sphere' (Chandler 2006a, p. 2; see also, Richmond et al. 2011). At the same time, the EU had long served as an institution on which hopes for more legitimacy in the internationally created public sphere could be focused, which was, according to Chandler (2006b, p, 35), mainly the case between 2000 and 2005, a phase of 'transition to EU "Ownership"'. It was hoped that the EU would be able to find a middle way, still ensuring a controlled transformation of the country and its political affairs, while being perceived as less imposing than the OHR and thus benefiting from a legitimacy bonus. This, however, failed, with the EU's popularity declining as people realized that the changes promoted by the EU were not significantly improving their lives. This represented yet another factor that considerably reduced people's trust in the public sphere and led to frustration with the political dynamics taking place in it. There is even an awareness in the international community that the popularity of the EU is in decline—mainly in the Federation—since it is not prepared to intervene as much as the OHR does.[4] The need to intervene in turn is contested among the population itself, with the Bosniaks generally being more positive towards OHR intervention than, for instance, the Bosnian Serbs or Croats (see Kostić 2007).

What we can observe in BiH more generally is a mutual shifting of responsibility for legitimacy deficits between the international community and local political elites. Often, when asking members of the international community in BiH about legitimacy issues in the country, they automatically refer to local conditions, such as issues with politicized media or corrupt politicians.[5] The World Bank, to cite one example, derives the lack of adequate social assistance schemes as well as a bad business environment in the country from the failure of the domestic system and elites to create better models of governance.[6]

In contrast, in the context of the long-lasting and ineffective attempts to form a government after the 2010 general elections, some political actors, mainly on the Bosniak side, and much less in RS, have called for the help of mainly the High Representative to use his power to act as an arbiter and help implement the election results in the cantons (see Kostić 2007).[7] Equally, in the context of constitutional reform, there is hope on the part of political actors—again, certainly much more in the Federation than in RS—that the international community will intervene to help design the reform process.[8] This reflects the extent to which responsibilities to create a legitimate system of governance are shifted between domestic and international elites, with neither of those actors being perceived as particularly legitimate in terms of their ability to connect to people's everyday experiences. Legitimacy is thus constructed from different perspectives, with different views of it. For instance, from the regional level, the

OHR is viewed as the last defence against local atavism, while from the local level, politicians and civil society actors often ruefully accept it may be needed but also argue it undermines their statebuilding process and their rights to autonomy.

But just as there is only low trust in politicians at best —mainly among the Bosniaks, there are frequent calls for the international community to engage in politics by sanctioning corrupt politicians[9] —the international community has a reputation for being distant from the everyday, not actually experiencing the day-to-day problems of their country of deployment.[10] This not only holds true for the bigger governing institutions, but also for smaller bodies. In order to get access to funding, these actors must change in accordance with various conditions (Belloni 2001, Fagan 2005, Mitchell and Kappler 2009), thereby risking losing touch with society. This is an experience shared by numerous organizations that have felt the need to adapt to this system to survive. The founder of a youth centre in Travnik mainly deplored the loss of a 'project spirit' when having to turn it into a funding application and transform the project according to the associated donor requirements.[11] Some local associations have, to a certain extent, managed to preserve their autonomy—the socio-critical artist association Ambrosia being one example of this —which has however often limited their access to funding and thus restricted the impact of their work.

The Hybrid, Semi-public Arena of the Cultural

Against this background, we need to ask what has happened to the processes of legitimacy—have they disappeared or rather moved to less public, less visible spaces? And do these versions compete with, block, reject, modify, or hybridize international versions of legitimacy? This section argues that rather than disappearing completely from society, legitimacy has been equipped with new means of survival. We may not find it exclusively in the public sphere, yet we can observe that it has been moved to what I call 'semi-public' spheres or arenas, where it has been revived and modified to make sense locally. In these spheres, we find a mutual penetration of the public and the private or the everyday, where the latter makes sense in the former and vice versa.

This runs counter the argument of Sarajlić-Maglić (2010, p. 57), who claims that 'frustrations with political system are not channeled into public action but into public apathy and resignation', pointing to a very common discourse in BiH, which accuses particularly young people of not engaging with the public sphere. In contrast, this paper suggests that there may be apathy in the public sphere, yet this only represents the surface of society, while we find manifestations of agency and legitimacy in semi-public spheres which connect much more closely to the lives of people and thus resist the legitimacy deficits in the public arena. This is in line with Boris Buden's (2003) argument, which situates the transformation of public space in a framework of cultural subversion, claiming that social change must be viewed as a transgressive (rather than dialectical) practice. In that context, Buden (2003) claims that '[p]ublic space... is not the site of political change as it once—in a very profound way—used to be'.

Having this in mind, I suggest that the locus of everyday politics as well as everyday legitimacy has partly moved away from the externalized public sphere, towards new arenas of contestation, conflict and negotiation, which form the very basis of alternative legitimacy structures in a local context through their ability to absorb the private. In this context, Andrea Cornwall (2004, p. 76) speaks of 'invited spaces', which bring together heterogeneous actors shaped by differences in status, 'who might relate very differently if they met in other settings'. Cultural spaces in BiH can be considered 'invited spaces' according to this definition. Indeed, what we can see with a lot of cultural institutions, whether those are formal or informal, is that they create spaces in which people can gather, which would not necessarily be possible in the public sphere, which is shaped by the power of the strongest, as well as ethnic divisions. However, a focus on theatres, concerts, galleries, choirs and so forth reflects the extent to which the users of such spaces can relate in alternative ways beyond the context of the public sphere. In that sense, 'invited spaces' change the dynamics of social relationships. Their accessibility may be limited in terms of only addressing an interested (mainly critical and alternative) mass, but at the same time they create a feeling of ownership, of 'being welcome', for their ('invited') members. Against this background, legitimacy has moved to semi-public arenas, constituted as invited spaces, which have developed structures connecting to people's everyday lives.

Indeed, cultural actors such as theatres deal closely with issues connected to social life in BiH. A dramaturgist of the Youth Theatre in Sarajevo, for instance, emphasized that one of the first questions when thinking about a future performance is always to what extent it will connect to people and their social experiences.[12] Numerous theatre directors, producers and dramaturgists interviewed in different parts of the country confirmed that their performances tend follow social issues as they are at stake in a given social situation. A programme director of the international theatre festival MESS explained the necessity of connecting with 'our society' in terms of talking about topical social problems, such as paedophilia.[13] To be able to communicate such ideas, they often use metaphors of the family as a symbol of society,[14] a clear integration of the private and the everyday. Again, this increases the feeling of belonging to and ownership of a space by the creators as well as the audience of that space. This reflects the extent to which the cultural sphere has the ability to make processes which appear distant and meaningless in the public sphere touchable in private spheres in terms of connecting them to people's lives. In that sense, the public and the private become closely intertwined, and cultural actors often link the meaning of politics in the public sphere to their meanings for people's identities.[15]

The Centre for Interdisciplinary Research of Visual Culture, for instance, has labelled politically sensitive and contested buildings, such as the highly fortified new American embassy in Sarajevo, to show their resistance to what they call 'visual pollution' of BiH's cultural landscape and its implications for people's everyday experiences.[16] This represents a way of personalizing the political, and it is easier to connect to people who feel there is a relationship between the political and their own lives. As a result, legitimacy can be re-situated in a personalized sphere, with cultural arenas serving as tools by which this re-situation can be realized. The connection between the political and the personal is particularly evident in the case of the multi-religious choir Pontanima, based in Sarajevo. Despite the religious and ethnic cleavages in the country, this choir represents a space in which people from diverse backgrounds can come together, which, following Cornwall's argument, would not be possible in the public sphere due to their different backgrounds. However, in the arena of the choir, otherwise conflicting social relations can be re-configured and personalized. The identities that are relevant in the public sphere (i.e. mainly ethnic ones) do not matter in the sphere of the choir, where it is all about personal relations.[17] A film producer who made a documentary about Pontanima considers the cohesion of the choir derives from the intense feelings it involves: its traumatic element, and at the same time its members' motivation and passion for the common project.[18] The choir, comprising about 20–40 active members, is renowned across the country. Numerous people have told me that they were deeply touched, not only by the music, but also by the courage of the members in performing cross-religious music. The reconciliation of Muslim, Christian, Jewish and other cultural markers is not common in the public sphere, but becomes a possibility in the choir's concert and rehearsal venues.

Not only do many of the semi-public cultural arenas personalize social and political relations, but, due to the negative perceptions of the political sphere and the associated lack of legitimacy, many cultural agencies place emphasis on not being perceived as political. The Centre for Culture in Travnik, although mainly funded by the municipality and thus necessarily having to cooperate with local authorities, emphasizes that it is not involved in any kind of political work, that it is not interested in nationalist ideologies, but rather in working professionally on its projects.[19] Along similar lines, the founder of the youth centre Alter Art emphasizes that the centre does not follow any nationalistic ideology, but is more interested in educating young people for free thinking.[20] Even a student radio station in Sarajevo emphasizes its deviation from the common political practices in the country, in which media and politicians work hand in hand, while the student radio station is trying to work differently, more independently and responding to the needs of its audience, i.e. the students.[21]

However, the statement of many cultural actors claiming that they are not engaging in the political sphere does not mean that they are not political. On the contrary, such actors create a critical (i.e. political) mass and thus use their transformative potential in their semi-public arenas to impact on structures of legitimacy, i.e. the way in which people perceive legitimate order as well as what kind of social contract they envisage, by evoking a critical consciousness. This is made possible by the fact that such organizations penetrate both the public and the private, and can therefore act as translators between them, hybridizing those spheres according to the needs of their audiences. It cannot in fact be argued that the cultural scene is free of politics in a broad sense. It has been suggested that BiH's political situation is clearly reflected in the cultural sector—an indicator of which is the fact that the war constituted a dramatic rupture not only in the country's political system, but at the same time also in its cultural life.[22] The president of the arts association Protok in Banja Luka suggested that its work is complementary and alternative to existing institutions, while the practice of the arts and artists refers critically to society and socio-political processes.[23] We can therefore observe that semi-public spheres are creating a kind of 'parallel world' to the public sphere, a world in which politics are made accessible to the users of this space, who then, rather than withdrawing from such processes, find different ways of engaging with them.

It is then in such spaces that disrupted social relations can be restored and implicit change becomes thinkable. In this context, the youth theatre in Sarajevo aims to change and educate people, at the same time emphasizing that this is very different from political processes in the public sphere, which 'does not give us enough, it does not give us enough space for thinking individually'.[24] Indeed, it is quite obvious that theatres have developed their own means of changing society. The theatre festival MESS, for instance, once featured a performance written by Oliver Frljić, a rather dark and violent story about the breakup of Yugoslavia. This was so intense that some people left or even attacked the actors, yet many others emphasized that the play really represented the anger they felt themselves and thus had a huge impact on them.[25] This reflects the impact the cultural arena can have on people in terms of establishing close connections with them, making them part of that sphere and including them in the processes that happen there. In this vein, cultural arenas are not only parallel worlds to the public sphere, but they also act as connectors between spheres. Centres such as the cultural youth centre Omladinski Kulturni Centar (OKC) Abrašević in Mostar or the youth centre in Srebrenica regularly organize public festivals during the course of which they connect their agendas to issues concerning the wider community. The 'Art in Divided Cities' festival in Mostar addressed the local community in terms of touching upon topics of everyday relevance in Mostar. This concerned the use of public space, its infrastructures, actors and so forth. Similarly, the Sarajevo Film Festival, the Sarajevo Winter Festival and the Mediterranean Film Festival in Široki Brijeg represent spaces in which public and private experiences can be reconfigured, at the same time addressing a wide audience. Indeed, the website of the Široki Brijeg festival claims that '[w]ithin the last ten years we have succeeded to create an atmosphere in which no one feels alienated, inferior or less invited to be a part of the event'.[26]

At the same time, the semi-public spaces that numerous cultural actors create work differently from the public spaces in which political actors operate. In this context, the director of the youth centre in Srebrenica suggested: 'I am not a politician, we have a different way of changing.'[27] Their way of changing consists of providing a space for young people where they can be creative and communicate their needs. In that sense, the tools of connecting to the users and creators (often people are in both roles) of the cultural arena differ radically from what would be acceptable in the public sphere. As the PR manager of the Museum for Contemporary Arts in Banja Luka pointed out, their work in the contemporary scene is very political, social as well as provocative. She quoted the example of a Serbian artist hosted by the museum who used real animal organs to create a cross—this was to shock and provoke people, but at the same time to force them to make a personal judgement about controversial topics, which tend to be avoided in public discourses.[28]

It becomes clear that, despite some overlaps, the audiences of the public and the cultural arena differ significantly from one another. This is related to the quality of the cultural scene as an 'invited space', a sphere in which ownership is created, which is accessible to a very different audience. The Museum for Contemporary Arts in Banja Luka, for instance, places emphasis on attracting all kinds of people, not just the social, cultural or political elites, claiming that 'the museum should be a place for everyone'.[29] In contrast to that, the arts association Sarajevo Center for Contemporary Art (SCCA) quite specifically speaks to a marginalized group of people, aiming to advocate for social minorities and their needs.[30] This is clearly linked to the idea of being able to change society with the help of arts and culture, since it is assumed that social problems are reflected in arts as well.[31] Aiming to provide a space for minorities and the marginalized of society, the youth centre OKC Abrašević in Mostar provides an alternative space in which people from the margins of society can come together without prejudice and participate in discourses, which is often denied in the public sphere.[32] This holds equally true for the arts centre Alter Art, which aims to create a creative space for young people, where they can express their opinions without restrictions,[33] which, again, would be subject to social censorship in the public space. Given that neither Travnik nor Mostar have a cinema, the cultural spaces of those towns serve as a rather popular venue, especially for young people.

The approach of numerous cultural spaces in connecting to all kinds of people means that people's engagement and motivation in this arena are much higher than in the public sphere, which tends to be shaped by frustration and resignation. It has indeed been suggested that people in Travnik are very involved in cultural activities, linked to a feeling of 'naš grad, naš rad, naša kultura' (our city, our work, our culture).[34] This feeling of ownership is due to the proximity of the cultural arena to people's lives, while the comparatively high degree of legitimacy is linked to feelings of trust and participation as well as the connection to the everyday, which makes the users of that space believe that there is a potential in arts to bring about social and political change, even though this may be on a very subtle level. Engagement in educational terms, mainly through theatres and films, is part of this change, just as much as the development of platforms on which the meanings of peace and social life can be discussed. The author has, for instance, witnessed a book presentation held during the Sarajevo Winter Festival in which the audience (about 60 people cramped into a tiny room) was emotionally touched in such a way that they connected the political and social messages of the book to their lives as well as discovering commonalities between their lives which they may not have expected. Therefore, we can observe that the audience of the semi-public cultural sphere is very different from that of the ethnicized, non-private, competitive public space, including the non-professional, the ordinary people, the marginalized and the contextualized selves.

The fact that the cultural arena gives space to the contextualized subject explains why this space is not homogeneous, but contested and fragmented through the encounter of a variety of subjectivities. It can be argued that this sphere is a highly fluid and flexible one, changing with the users involved in the space, which in turn points to its quality as a receiving platform. It can indeed been said that cultural activities help create open spaces of interaction between people. For instance, Pravo Ljudski, a human rights film festival, aims to create an open space for people in which they can get access to information and can move on a platform of discussion.[35] This is based on the assumption that in order to create peace, people need a common space where they can discuss and agree on the foundations of their social life.[36] In that sense, the arenas of culture serve as microcosms in which different versions of peace can be negotiated, tested, developed and modified. At the same time, the ownership of such processes rests with the users of that space, i.e. the subject in its everyday, subjective context.

We can therefore claim that legitimacy translates as ownership and vice versa, with the cultural arena providing platforms of discourse on which legitimacy and authority as well as associated rules and norms can be constantly renegotiated in subtle ways. In practice, this has concrete implications for the work of a number of grassroots organizations. The music rehearsal rooms in the youth centre Alter Art, for instance, were completely refurbished by the youth from the community, which created a strong feeling of ownership of that space and is still keeping them together as a community.[37] Similarly, the cultural youth centres in Srebrenica and in Mostar were (re-)built by their current users, who still feel that the respective centre is their second home, in which they can express themselves freely and discuss any topic connected to social life. The OKC Abrašević in Mostar organized a festival on 'Defence of Public Space, Defence of our Future'. Not only did this festival promote diverse cultural events, but it also provided a space in which people could sit together informally and discuss problems with the current post-war situation as well as options for the future of the city and their lives.[38] The same is true for the Duplex Gallery in Sarajevo, where the owner has created a small exhibition space for local artists. This space seems symbolically outside the public sphere—it is hidden and hard to find—but at the same time this has developed into a vibrant arena for those who know about it. Artists frequently gather in the backyard of the gallery to discuss social issues, problems in their everyday lives and the political realities in BiH.[39]

These dynamics reflect the shifting of legitimacy structures into the semi-public sphere, where a variety of actors create connections to people and their private everyday contexts. If we remind ourselves of the notion of legitimacy as a social construction, it becomes clear that there are a number of competing legitimacies at play in the cultural arena. Indeed, legitimacy in terms of who is trusted to be a legitimate promoter of social change is constantly renegotiated by a variety of actors, but those debates are given a platform in the cultural arena. The latter represents a sphere in which actors can configure differently from the ways that would be possible in the public sphere. In that sense, the local scene serves as an interesting example of how, when disintegrating in the public sphere, legitimacy can be re-configured in alternative circles to re-establish the connection between governing structures and people's everyday lives. This suggests that the internationally imposed and political elite-implemented peace is problematic as a result of its inability to account for the private and the failure to translate this into the public sphere. As a result, legitimacy in the cultural arena emerges from its ability to hybridize public and private concerns, which connect people's experiences to political action and thus create a feeling of ownership.

Conclusion

This article has pointed to the legitimacy deficits in the public sphere in BiH, resulting from the distance between the governing political elites and international community on the one hand, and the population on the other. This has been linked to the creation of a distance between the public and the private, while the everyday has been limited in its ability to penetrate an externalized public sphere. The paper has illustrated how this has led to a shifting of legitimacy to semi-public spheres, the cultural arena being one example of this, in which structures of legitimacy are reconstituted in alternative, more fragmented ways. The cultural arena has been able to gain more legitimacy through its capacity to hybridize the public and the private. It needs to be said that this does not mean that the cultural sphere enjoys legitimacy from the perspective of all sectors of society—indeed its impact may be considered a limited one—or that it is the only alternative sphere that enjoys legitimacy. However, the cultural arena shows us that legitimacy does not merely disappear, but that it moves to other spheres and platforms. Cultural arenas can thus be considered microcosms of legitimacy for the users of these arenas, creating alternative structures of identification and social configuration that might not be thinkable in the public sphere. This involves, for instance, common cross-ethnic or interreligious projects as well as the presentation of artwork in provocative ways.

At the same time, it is important to be aware of the fact that although semi-public spaces differ from the public spaces, they are not completely isolated from them. Instead, cultural spaces are certainly regulated, restrained and controlled by the public sphere—one must not forget that the majority of cultural activities in BiH are sponsored by the state or municipality and are therefore accountable to public authorities to a certain extent. Yet, in a sense, semi-public spaces are also enabled by the deficits of the public space, through their ability to find ways of modifying existing or external concepts of legitimacy through their connection to the everyday. These dynamics are particularly interesting in the peacebuilding context, since they show us that local actors have subtly managed what international actors have been struggling with for a long time: the reconstruction of legitimacy in a war-torn country. Certainly, these alternative legitimacy structures might not necessarily please the political elites and the international community that would much rather see legitimacy emerge in the public sphere of the state—which would most likely also be a desirable goal for most of the population. Yet, due to a failure to achieve this, new actors have been empowered and taken over functions of the public spheres on their own terms. Against the background of a lack of a broad social contract between national and international elites and the population, small and informal social contracts have been established in the cultural sphere, in which people's everyday needs are addressed and given a voice. The resulting processes of peace and legitimacy have thus been fragmented and moved to the margins of society, which is problematic due to a lack of a central platform of debate. However, this has resulted in a chance for marginalized actors to get included in smaller arenas, where they can contribute to a newly emerging social contract with their own experiences and needs.

Acknowledgements

Many thanks to Oliver Richmond as well as two anonymous reviewers for their very constructive comments on this article.

Notes on Contributor

Stefanie Kappler is a post-doctoral teaching fellow at Liverpool Hope University. Her research focuses on EU peacebuilding in Bosnia-Herzegovina in the light of the local agencies that resist and challenge it.

Notes

1. http://www.ohr.int/dpa/default.asp?content_id=372 [Accessed 1 April 2011].
2. Confidential source, personal interview, Banja Luka, 27 April 2010.
3. Mark Wheeler, OHR, personal interview, Sarajevo, 16 March 2010.

4   Confidential source, international community, personal interview, Sarajevo, 3 March 2011.
5   Confidential source, international community, personal interview, Sarajevo, 3 March 2011. This mainly came out during five field trips to BiH between 2008 and 2011.
6   Marco Mantovanelli, World Bank, personal interview, Sarajevo, 7 March 2011.
7   Nermina Zaimović-Uzunović, SDP, personal interview, Sarajevo, 7 March 2011. This source can certainly not be read as representative in that the interviewee is a member of a political party that pursues certain goals. Yet it is illustrative of some claims being made from the side of the Federation.
8   Nermina Zaimović-Uzunović, SDP, personal interview, Sarajevo, 7 March 2011.
9   Darko Saracević, Alter Art, personal interview, Travnik, 2 March 2011.
10 Pierre Courtin, Duplex Gallery, personal interview, Sarajevo, 23 April 2010.
11 Darko Saracević, Alter Art, personal interview, Travnik, 2 March 2011.
12 Aida Pilav, Pozoriste Mladih Sarajevo, personal interview, Sarajevo, 31 March 2010.
13 Selma Spahić, MESS Sarajevo and National Theatre Zenica, personal interview, Sarajevo, 3 March 2011.
14 Ibid.
15 Aida Bucalović, Center for Interdisciplinary Research of Visual Culture, personal interview, Sarajevo, 21 April 2010.
16 Ibid.
17 The author visited the choir rehearsals during a couple of months in spring 2010.
18 Namik Kabil, film producer, personal interview, Sarajevo, 14 April 2010.
19 Vildana Kalčo, Center za Kulturu, personal interview, Travnik, 2 March 2011.
20 Darko Saracević, Alter Art, personal interview, Travnik, 2 March 2011.
21 Mirza Ajnadčić, EFM student radio, personal interview, Sarajevo, 7 March 2011.
22 Vildana Kalčo, Center za Kulturu, personal interview, Travnik, 2 March 2011.
23 Radenko Milak, Protok, email conversation, 4 June 2010.
24 Aida Pilav, Pozoriste Mladih Sarajevo, personal interview, Sarajevo, 31 March 2010.
25 Selma Spahić, MESS Sarajevo and National Theatre Zenica, personal interview, Sarajevo, 3 March 2011.
26 http://www.mff.ba/mff_x_ofestivalu.asp [Accessed 18 September 2011].
27 Milena Nikolić, Youth Centre Srebrenica, personal interview, Srebrenica, 2 April 2010.
28 Branka Šestić, Muzej Savremene Umjetnosti RS, personal interview, Banja Luka, 27 April 2010.
29 Ibid.
30 Asja Hafner, scca/pro.ba, personal interview, Sarajevo, 16 April 2010.
31 Ibid.
32 Katie Hampton, OKC Abrašević, personal interview, Mostar, 18 March 2010.
33 Darko Saracević, Alter Art, personal interview, Travnik, 2 March 2011.
34 Vildana Kalčo, Center za Kulturu, personal interview, Travnik, 2 March 2011.
35 Kumjana Novakova, Pravo Ljudski, personal interview, Sarajevo, 9 April 2010.
36 Ibid.
37 Darko Saracević, Alter Art, personal interview, Travnik, 2 March 2011.
38 The author attended parts of the festival at OKC Abrašević, 'Defence of Public Space, Defence of our Future', Mostar, 15 April 2010.
39 The author has been present at such occasions. Also: Pierre Courtin, Duplex Gallery, personal interview, Sarajevo, 23 April 2010.

References

Arendt, H., 1958. *The human condition*. Chicago, IL: University of Chicago Press.
Arendt, H., 1967. *The origins of totalitarianism*. London: Allen and Unwin.

Beacroft, M., 2007. Defining political theory: an Arendtian approach to difference in the public realm. *Politics*, 27 (1), 40–47.

Belloni, R., 2001. Civil society and peacebuilding in Bosnia and Herzegovina. *Journal of peace research*, 38 (2), 163–180.

Belloni, R., 2004. Peacebuilding and consociational electoral engineering in Bosnia and Herzegovina. *International peacekeeping*, 11 (2), 334–353.

Berman, N., 2010. Intervention in a 'divided world': axes of legitimacy. *In*: H. Charlesworth and J.-M. Coicaud, eds. *Fault lines of international legitimacy*. New York: Cambridge University Press.

Boutros-Ghali, B., 1996. *An agenda for democratization*. New York: United Nations.

Boyd, S.B., 1997. *Challenging the public/private divide: feminism, law, and public policy*. Toronto, Buffalo and London: University of Toronto Press.

Buden, B., 2003. *Public space as translation process* [online]. Available from: http://www.republicart.net/disc/realpublicspaces/buden03_en.htm [Accessed 28 March 2011].

Chandler, D., 2002. Anti-corruption strategies and democratization in Bosnia-Herzegovina. *Democratization*, 9 (2), 101–120.

Chandler, D., 2006a. Introduction: peace without politics? *In*: D. Chandler, ed. *Peace without politics? Ten years of international state-building in Bosnia*. London and New York: Routledge.

Chandler, D., 2006b. From Dayton to Europe. *In*: D. Chandler, ed. *Peace without politics? Ten years of international state-building in Bosnia*. London and New York: Routledge.

Clark, I., 2007. *Legitimacy in international society*. Oxford: Oxford University Press.

Coicaud, J.-M., 2010. Legitimacy, across borders and over time. *In*: H. Charlesworth and J.-M. Coicaud, eds. *Fault lines of international legitimacy*. New York: Cambridge University Press.

Coleman, K.P., 2007. *International organisations and peace enforcement. The politics of international legitimacy*. New York: Cambridge University Press.

Cornwall, A., 2004. Spaces for transformation? Reflections on issues of power and difference in participation in development. *In*: S. Hickey and G. Mohan, eds. *Participation. From tyranny to transformation?* London: Zed Books.

Diamond, L., 1999. *Developing democracy: toward consolidation*. Baltimore, MD: Johns Hopkins University Press.

Divjak, B. and Pugh, M., 2008. The political economy of corruption in Bosnia and Herzegovina. *International peacekeeping*, 15 (3), 373–386.

Donais, T., 2003. The political economy of stalemate: organised crime, corruption and economic deformation in post-Dayton Bosnia. *Conflict, security and development*, 3 (3), 359–382.

Fagan, A., 2005. Civil society in Bosnia ten years after Dayton. *International peacekeeping*, 12 (3), 406–419.

Foucault, M., 1980. *Power/knowledge*. New York: Pantheon Books.

Fox, J., 1999. The influence of religious legitimacy on grievance formation by ethno-religious minorities. *Journal of peace research*, 36 (3), 289–307.

Franck, T.M., 1990. *The power of legitimacy among nations*. New York and Oxford: Oxford University Press.

Horwitz, M.J., 1982. The history of the public/private distinction. *University of Pennsylvania law review*, 130 (6), 1423–1428.

Kappler, S. and Richmond, O.P., 2011. Peacebuilding in Bosnia and Herzegovina: resistance or emancipation? *Security dialogue*, 42 (3), 261–278.

Kostić, R., 2007. *Ambivalent peace: external nation-building, threatened identity and reconciliation in Bosnia-Herzegovina*. Thesis (PhD). Department of Peace and Conflict Research, Uppsala University.

Mitchell, A. and Kappler, S., 2009. Transformative civil society? The ethics and mechanisms of EU peace-building in Bosnia and Northern Ireland. Paper presented at the Millennium Annual Conference, London School of Economics, October.

National Democratic Institute, 2010. Public opinion poll Bosnia and Herzegovina (BiH) August 2010 [online]. Available from: http://www.ndi.org/files/NDI_Bosnia_Poll_Report_August_2010.pdf [Accessed 2 April 2011].

Pugh, M., 2002. Political economy in Bosnia and Herzegovina: the spoils of peace. *Global governance*, 8 (4), 467–482.

Richmond, O.P., 2011. *A post-liberal peace*. New York and London: Routledge.

Richmond, O.P., Björkdahl, A. and Kappler, S., 2011. The emerging EU peacebuilding framework: confirming or transcending liberal peacebuilding? *Cambridge review of international affairs*, 24 (3), 449–469.

Sarajlić-Maglić, D., 2010. Can BiH elites run the state? *In*: Heinrich Böll Foundation, Office for Bosnia and Herzegovina, ed. *Bosnia and Herzegovina: between EU-integration toolbox and international community's exit strategy*. Sarajevo: Heinrich Böll Foundation.

Schwarz, R., 2005. Post-conflict peacebuilding: the challenges of security, welfare and representation. *Security dialogue*, 36 (4), 429–446.

Simonsen, S.G., 2005. Addressing ethnic divisions in post-conflict institution-building: lessons from recent cases. *Security dialogue*, 36 (3), 297–318.

Uhlin, A., 2010. Democratic legitimacy of transnational actors: mapping out the conceptual terrain. *In*: E. Erman and A. Uhlin, eds. *Legitimacy beyond the state? Re-examining the democratic credentials of transnational actors*. Basingstoke: Palgrave Macmillan.

United Nations Development Programme (UNDP), 2010. *Early warning system 2010*. Sarajevo: UNDP.

Weintraub, J., 1997. The theory and politics of the public/private distinction. *In*: J. Weintraub and K. Kumar, eds. *Public and private in thought and practice. Perspectives on a grand dichotomy*. Chicago: University of Chicago Press.

Health, Conflict, Stability and Statebuilding: A House Built on Sand?

Stuart Gordon

Increasingly, the purpose of third party health interventions in fragile states has become linked to statebuilding agendas in order to build government through health programmes. However, there is only limited data to support the efficacy of such an assumption. Indeed, this approach may instead invert the desired outcome of social legitimacy and undermine the rationale for which it is intended. This paper examines the strategic response from donors vis-à-vis the objective of statebuilding, and concludes that new research is required. It concludes that until there is empirically based evidence of the benefits of health interventions for statebuilding, the goals of health interventions should remain fixed primarily on improving health indicators instead.

The purpose of third party health interventions in fragile states has diversified beyond the traditional concern for the relief of suffering (Nye 2002, Harris 2004, Fidler 2005, Horton 2007, Owen and Roberts 2005, Thieren 2007, Feldbaum and Michaud 2010). Increasingly the health literature is occupied by the potential for enhanced governance and capacity for service delivery *within* the health sector to contribute to building the wider institutions of state, reducing the potential for conflict (MacQueen et al. 1997) and shaping the attitudes of beneficiaries towards governments and/or intervening military forces. In other words, health is advanced as a means of legitimating the evolving state to the people over whom it seeks dominion. Health then becomes a tool with which to foster respect for the state by making it relevant to ordinary people's lives and establishing a process which constructs a social contract from which stability might derive. Health interventions have therefore become firmly enmeshed in liberal statebuilding models. In Afghanistan and Iraq health has become not only a part of this wider endeavour but is also widely portrayed as a pillar of the counter insurgency and stabilization strategies (Cramer and Goodhand 2002, Killcullen 2005, Jones et al. 2008, Marine Corps 2007, Utzinger and Weiss 2007, US Department of State 2009, Gordon 2011a). This is frequently characterized as a process of 'securitization' of assistance strategies—or co-option and distortion by foreign and security policy elites (Cramer and Goodhand 2002, Wilder 2010).

However, this article suggests that the process is far more complex and not simply related to the demand for instruments for enhancing the performance legitimacy of the state. Rather, the pressures relate to a range of considerations resulting from our growing understanding of the impact that conflict has specifically on health systems. Single issue programmes such as child immunization, feeding programmes or the creation and operation of specialized facilities such as emergency field hospitals are increasingly characterized as insufficient. The health literature reflects a recognition that reductions in mortality and morbidity rates require the pursuit of holistic strategies aimed at strengthening health systems as a whole. In turn, this encourages complex interventions which require considerable efforts across the international donor community in order to maintain coherence. As a whole, such pressures lead to an increasing propensity to strengthen health systems. Furthermore, the choice of strategy in 'stabilization' operations, namely an increasing propensity to deliver external health interventions through strengthening the state's capacity to manage public health policy and utilizing non-state actors for delivery (Palmer and Strong 2006) increases the probability that health interventions will have greater linkages with the statebuilding, fragile state and counterinsurgency agendas. The result has been the use of health service interventions as key components of efforts to build the performance legitimacy of the state rather than as valuable simply in terms of the overall health benefits. This paper explores these processes: examining how the impact of conflict on health systems has necessitated a statebuilding approach from health professionals and how this has exposed health interventions to capture by the liberal statebuilding and counterinsurgency agendas. It also asks where we are in terms of the evidence underpinning our understanding of how health interventions remedy state fragility through legitimating the state.

The impact of conflict on health outcomes is documented extensively (Pedersen 2002, WHO 2002, Coghlan *et al.* 2006, Newbrander *et al.* 2007, Rubenstein 2009, Levy and Sidel 2008, Panter-Brick 2010).

However, the mechanisms through which mortality and morbidity increase during conflict have frequently been overlooked, particularly in terms of their impact on the nature of health interventions and the association with the statebuilding agenda. Arguably conflict has an important impact on two issues: patient access to and the strength of health services in affected countries; and through increasing a population's vulnerability to disease vectors.

Conflict's Impact on the Health Service and the Disruption of Medical Programmes

In terms of the access to and the strength of health services the effects of conflict are most keenly felt through the displacement of key staff and the destruction of health infrastructure (Macrae and Leader 2000), as well as precipitating the breakdown of state policy and financing mechanisms

(Roberts *et al.* 2008, Zwi *et al.* 2008). Anthony Zwi (1991) also argues that it diverts political and elite attention and resources towards managing the conflict and investing in military and state survival functions rather than maintaining the health sector.

Health facilities and workers may also become targets for political reasons and this theme has been elaborated in several studies. Pavignani and Colombo in their 2001 work, for example, detail the way in which primary health care and education provision became important elements of the Mozambican government's social policy post-independence from Portuguese rule in 1975 (see also Cliff and Noormahomed 1988, Keane 1996). The targeting of health workers for political reasons—largely relating to disrupting the ability of the state to build legitimacy through connecting with the population—has also been recorded in a wide range of other conflicts: Chechnya, Nicaragua, Peru, Timor Leste, Sri Lanka (Nagai *et al.* 2007), Iraq, Afghanistan (Loevinsohn and Sayed 2008), Pakistan, the Philippines, Croatia and Bosnia, Kashmir, etc. (see Zivetz 2006, Levy and Sidel 2008). In addition to politically motivated targeting, a rapidly expanding literature highlights the way in which conflict destroys disease control and health programmes through reducing the resources for and disrupting access to vaccination programmes, diagnosis and treatment.

Vulnerability to Disease Vectors and the Disruption of Medical Programmes

Furthermore, population displacement increases population vulnerability—worsening hygiene, increasing overcrowding and facilitating the spread of communicable diseases. The impact of conflict on tuberculosis (TB) treatment, a major source of morbidity and mortality in some conflict states, provides a useful illustration of these broader processes (Tiwari *et al.* 2005, Coninz 2007) with authors such as Gele and Bjune (2010) arguing that escalating poverty and malnutrition increase the number of TB susceptible individuals but also deter infected and infectious patients from being diagnosed promptly and gaining treatment (see also Ponsar *et al.* 2009)—concluding that this process increases the number of infections through extending the infectious period—fuelling the large increases in TB infections that accompany open warfare.

Arguably, the principal dynamic increasing the indirect mortality and morbidity rates in conflict situations is the impact of conflict on the access to medical attention of population groups that require a complex of preventive, diagnostic, palliative and restorative care, partly explaining the trend towards more holistic approaches to health system strengthening in contemporary health programmes. Such pressures have coincided with the assumption that broadly focused health provision by the state is a key component of state legitimacy.

The Strategic Response from Donors: From the Sectoral to the State? From Projects and Badly Co-ordinated Aid to Health System Strengthening

There has also been a trend, driven by the aid effectiveness discourse, to address criticisms of disunity and the arbitrary duplication of resources focused around NGO capacity rather than local needs. Laurence and Poole (2005, p. 15) for example, suggest that a description of a typical intervention is that of

> donors funding NGOs to provide services, with the NGOs maintaining tightly vertical systems for monitoring and reporting on resources and financial management. A 'patchwork' of operations driven by competing donor priorities, processes and reporting requirements—this is sometimes organised by allocating certain districts to certain funders and/or NGOs.

Distortions also derive from overlapping or duplicative efforts on the part of donors and recipient states—reducing overall effectiveness and creating inefficiencies (Krug *et al.* 2002, Vergeer *et al.* 2009). Eldon *et al.* (2008) also point to the way in which international NGOs may distort health programming priorities—tending to focus more on visible deliverables such as facilities, infrastructure and single issue vertical programmes and suggesting a relative neglect of the less visible support capacities such as procurement, health information and policy framework development that might strengthen the health system as a whole and lead to more sustainable outcomes. Vergeer *et al.* (2009) echo this point, drawing attention to preferences of health practitioners for life saving interventions rather than focusing on sustainability or capacity-building. In contrast, health provision focused around the objective of legitimating the state favoured interdependent systems involving state institutions, policy frameworks, civil society and an array of non-state actors—NGOs and for-profit organizations. Within these frameworks humanitarian programmes are frequently described as providing structured vertical programmes such as child immunization or feeding programmes and specialized facilities such as emergency field hospitals, with some agencies pursuing broader objectives including mental and reproductive health, education, training and prevention strategies (Pavignani and Colombo 2001, Betsi *et al.* 2006).

Whilst practice may err on the side of life saving interventions, the academic and practitioner literature demonstrates a broad-based consensus that improvements in health system strengthening (HSS) facilitate far more significant improvements in health outcomes and, it is suggested, political legitimacy where it is often sorely lacking and much needed for the longer term objectives of state stability and durable peace. There is also considerable agreement on the requirement to devise national policy frameworks for health interventions at the earliest possible opportunity (Carlson *et al.* 2005). In addition, the increasing focus by donors on service delivery strategies as remedies for state fragility also derive from 'aid effectiveness' discourses (Macrae and Harmer 2004, Wheeler *et al.* 2006). The pursuit of the Millennium Development Goals (MDGs) in particular has encouraged a reconsideration of aid instruments and strategies that bypass the state (Leader and Colenso 2005)—largely because service delivery through quasi-humanitarian programmes have been viewed as lacking the scale and reach necessary to deliver the MDGs. This has spawned a debate around the relative merits of humanitarian and development assistance (Commins and Fenton 2007, Leader and Colenso 2005) with critics arguing that humanitarian action, particularly when it becomes a substitute for state service delivery, has the potential to undermine the state and sustainability more generally. However, this has to be weighed against the fact that humanitarian organizations are often the first agencies on the ground in fragile post-conflict states (Berry *et al.* 2004b) and offer both flexibility (Bornemisza and Zwi 2008) and a capacity to scale up responses in the absence of government capacity. These debates are, however, often complicated by the messy reality of interventions—where humanitarian NGOs are often willing to bypass the state on certain controversial issues (such as reproductive health and HIV) but would pragmatically work with and through the state on others (see Eldon *et al.* 2008). Despite the differences between declaratory positions and implementation strategies, authors such as Rubinstein (2009, pp. 3–4) argue compellingly that

> There exists a growing consensus that in many circumstances donors can best address the health crises stemming from war by moving as quickly as possible from providing emergency health services to supporting the capacity of the state's ministry of health to plan, implement and oversee a comprehensive and transparent system of health services grounded in primary care.

One of the ways in which donors (principally the World Bank, European Commission, European states, the Asia Development Bank and the US Agency for International Development) have sought to manage the overall coherence of their interventions and the transition from emergency relief to more sustainable forms of delivery is through establishing Basic Packages of Health Services (BPHS). Initially championed by the World Bank and piloted in Cambodia, the approach has also been attempted in Afghanistan (Peters *et al.* 2007, Hansen and Peters 2008), DRC, Southern Sudan, East Timor (ODI 2003), Liberia and Somalia (Fenton 2007, Pavanello and Darcy 2008) and involves the beneficiary state government and donors jointly contracting NGOs to provide primary care services with most of the available financial health resources allocated to it with a view to rapidly scaling up health services (Waldman 2006, 2007, Roberts *et al.* 2008).

Loevinsohn and Harding (2005, pp. 678–681) argue that its principal benefits are in terms of 'effectiveness, efficiency and equity'—potentially creating a cost-effective strategy that is most able to reduce mortality and morbidity and address issues of equity (see also Newbrander 2007, pp. 319–336). Similarly, other authors argue that the creation of a strategic framework for donors appears to facilitate greater aid effectiveness and coherence in their efforts as well as a process for addressing issues of equity in medical access. The reliance on NGOs is therefore generally described positively—offering speed, capacity and greater levels of health access equity than weak governments are generally able to deliver (Cometto 2006, p. 232; see also Roberts *et al*. 2008, pp. 57–64). Whilst there is little in the way of peer-reviewed evidence (notwithstanding Waldman *et al*. 2006, Waldman 2003), in the case of Afghanistan the government has drawn attention to a rapid scaling up of delivery with the Ministry of Public Health's (MOPH) Grants and Management Unit; concluding that by early 2005, two years after its inception, the BPHS had extended health care to 77 per cent of the population (Lancet 2005). In November 2009, Amin Fatimie (2009), Minister of Public Health of Afghanistan, announced that the BPHS covered around 85 per cent of Afghanistan's rural areas.

However, whilst BPHSs appear to have made significant contributions to the rapid extension of public services in fragile environments (Peters *et al*. 2007) there appears to be very limited peer-reviewed evidence on their broader effectiveness, particularly in terms of their impact on government legitimacy and the trade-offs arising from the reduced role for government in delivery.[1] Furthermore, there are clear risks. Whilst some might argue that the BPHS mechanisms are an interim measure pending the growth in government capacity, authors such as Palmer *et al*. (2005) warn of the potential for this to become a permanent feature of service provision, arguing that limiting the role of the government to that of 'decision maker' rather than 'deliverer' potentially reduces the capacity of the government to generate legitimacy through service delivery and may not have a particularly strong role in strengthening government.

The key point from the preceding analysis is that there are extraordinary internal pressures for health interventions to be constructed in terms of a liberal statebuilding discourse. These pressures are not simply externally imposed as part of a liberal or counter insurgency agenda. Rather they arise, to a large degree, from the profession's own view of what constitutes 'best practice'.

From Health System Strengthening to Legitimate States?

Rendering effective health service delivery for its own sake, then, has evolved into health provision as a dualism, able to generate political legitimacy through social care. Krug *et al*. (2002, p. 90), for example, provide a useful summary of these broader aspirations—arguing that the careful design of these

> health system building blocks—including the regulatory framework, resource allocation, financing, package of services, mode of delivery, human resource management, etc.—can build government capacity, promote social cohesion, and strengthen the social contract, thereby promoting state building and reducing the risks of conflict recurrence.

Rubenstein (2009) echoes this view, suggesting that the

> most commonly cited potential benefits of service delivery in post-conflict environments are that visible delivery enhances state legitimacy, strengthens the social contract and hence, promotes state building. Delivery of services can also

address underlying causes of conflict, i.e. social exclusion, and services such as health can be used as entry point for wider peace-building processes.

Eldon *et al.* (2008, p. 4), quoting Fritz and Menocal (2008), argue that statebuilding can be

> significantly enhanced by well-targeted, responsive international assistance to build capacity, institutions and legitimacy. They draw particular attention to the 'state–society compact' and its institutionalization through 'political process or accountability mechanisms through which the state and society reconcile their expectations of one another.

The health literature is not alone in stressing the significance of what could be described as strategic frameworks. Since 9/11 the fragile state agenda has generally assumed increased significance both from a security perspective (as a major driver of instability and insecurity) and as a key challenge to delivering the Millennium Development Goals (USAID 2005, Whaites 2009). Pavanello and Darcy (2008) argue that this paralleled the growing interest in 'service delivery' that was itself placed at the heart of the development agenda in 2004 by the *World Bank* 2004 *World Development Report: Making Services Work for the Poor.* As a consequence of these changes, service delivery strategies—particularly in the areas of health care, education, water/sanitation and rural infrastructure—were increasingly conceived as the critical building blocks in developing the state's performance legitimacy in a way that was sufficient both for the fragile state's immediate survival and for its longer term growth (DFID 2005, Newbrander 2007, Menocal 2009). As such, authors such as Pavanello and Darcy have argued that service delivery is linked to state fragility and could have broader transformative effects in terms of statebuilding—impacting particularly on the relationship between citizens and governments (see also Berry *et al.* 2004a, Newbrander 2007).

This emphasis on service delivery as a means of building and thence legitimating the state has obvious implications for the health sector. Whilst there had already been recognition that the strengthening of health system governance processes and institutions could have a positive impact on health outcomes (Brinkerhoff 2008), the statebuilding discourses have encouraged the belief that health sector interventions could deliver a much more ambitious range of 'super-ordinate' goals: building social capital, state legitimacy and stimulating the growth of peace processes as well as broader state functions that had the potential to consolidate the processes and institutions of fragile states.

The Evidence Base: Does Building Health Systems Legitimate States?

Whilst there is considerable agreement within *both* the peer-reviewed and practitioner literatures that it is *reasonable* to expect health interventions to support wider statebuilding outcomes, improve government legitimacy and potentially even to reduce conflict, there is also almost unanimous consensus within the peer-reviewed literature that the evidence base is weak and there is still a requirement for additional research. Eldon *et al.* (2008) suggest that there is frequent and recurring criticism that the evidence base tends to be anecdotal or inconclusive and possibly reflects 'organizational interests'. They conclude that there is a need for more 'detailed empirical and field based research' and suggest that there is very little evidence either way. They add that

> links between the health sector and wider state-building might include connections to other Ministries and core state functions such as financial management and local government decision-making—however the evidence is contradictory. Some observers draw attention to the weaknesses of ministries of health compared to other ministries, while others suggest that achievements in the health sector can serve as a model for other sectors. Evidence from the field was equally contradictory and inconclusive. (Eldon *et al.* 2008, p. 22)

Furthermore, this study suggests that despite the profusion of declaratory statements in the practitioner literature, there appear to be very few health programmes that systematically and explicitly address issues of state stewardship, stabilization or statebuilding outcomes within their programme design. Perhaps surprisingly, even candidates such as the International Security Assistance Force (ISAF) health programme in Helmand, Afghanistan and the Opération des Nations unies au Congo (ONUC) health support plans in the eastern Congo appear to have little or no direct declaratory role in terms of stabilization and *wider* statebuilding outcomes. Both are pursued by health professionals largely for the sake of health outcomes and have no inbuilt mechanisms for monitoring the impact on government legitimacy. A review of recent Department for International Development (DFID) programme documentation by this author also highlighted the elusive nature of health governance and capacity indicators and a requirement to develop clear and measurable indicators of progress in the areas of the 'superordinate goals' and the general lack of investment in systematic monitoring and evaluation of programmes in these areas (Gordon *et al.* 2010).

Perhaps one of the strongest assertions in the practitioner (or 'grey') literature is that service delivery interventions may contribute to peace and security (WHO 2006, MOD 2010). In very limited cases, health may have been one factor in cementing a peace process and clearly the health of a population is essential to economic development—with economic growth frequently being associated with a greater propensity towards more sustainable forms of peace. However, despite the intensity of assertions and the numerous theories of change associated with ideas such as 'health as a bridge for peace' (HBP) (see Cahill 1987, Guerra de Macedo 1994, Gutlove 1998, Rodriguez-Garcia *et al.* 2001, Santa Barbara and MacQueen 2004, WHO 2005, 2006, Rushton and McInnes 2006, Gunn 2009, Hess and Pfeiffer 1999, Gordon 2011a) there are no systematic evaluations of the effectiveness of health interventions in driving peace negotiations or cementing subsequent agreements (Vaas 2001, p. 1020) or of the impact of capacity-building interventions in health departments (Zivetz 2006) on the growth of state legitimacy. This finding was paralleled by Colin McInnes and Kelley Lee (2006, p. 18) who concluded that:

> the evidentiary base appears slim and overly reliant on anecdotal evidence rather than rigorous and systematic empirical work. Moreover, there has been little conceptual work done on key questions including: what works and why? What conditions are susceptible to such an approach? What level and form of health investment is required? When might it backfire and allow a conflict to continue? Can it be used to assist in ending conflicts, or just in post-conflict reconstruction? And can it be used to prevent conflict?

Rubenstein's 2009 study, concludes in a similar vein, arguing that there

> is very little evidence on the impact of service delivery initiatives on producing a peace dividend, or providing the basis for longer-term sustainable reform. This may be because of the small number of available cases, and the limited availability of quantitative and qualitative information, as well as the difficulties of data collection in post-conflict environments.

Waldman (2006) echoes these findings, asserting 'there is little evidence in general and none in DRC to suggest that even major improvements in health service delivery will be singularly important to the consolidation of the peace process'. Furthermore, the view that service provision can manufacture legitimacy for a government in the absence of peace and security (implicit in the US approach in Afghanistan) does not appear to be supported by the available literature (Sabri *et al.* 2007, Hansen *et al.* 2008). Rubinstein (2009) reinforced these findings in his analysis of what he calls US military 'health diplomacy'—which he describes as 'health interventions as a means of achieving strategic objectives in stabilization contexts such as Afghanistan and Iraq, while at the same time aiming for a positive impact on the health sector as a whole'. He concludes that

> there is little evidence to suggest that even major improvements in health services delivery have proved a singularly important factor in the consolidation of the peace process or in the successful passage from transitional government to a more stable political environment. This may be because, as other experts suggest, the legitimacy of the state depends on much more than the delivery of services and that stabilization, therefore, requires a more multi-pronged and multi-layered approach.

Despite the lack of systematic empirical evidence, some donors have already responded to the security imperative. In DRC and South Sudan, for example, the United States Agency for International Development (USAID) shifted its health provision efforts away from areas with little or no health care to more unstable areas in an effort to consolidate the peace process—arguing that this short term focus improved the longer term prospects of health by stopping conflict or reducing the potential for renewal. However there is 'little evidence … that this strategy was particularly effective' (Waldman 2006). Such an approach also introduces the potential for distortions—focusing on visible infrastructure, geographical areas or issues that are perhaps related to the risk of renewed conflict or imperatives to build state legitimacy in some way rather than focusing on health need or capacity development within the system as a whole. This may also generate inequities and resentments in the excluded areas and lead us to the tentative conclusion that it may be extremely difficult to simultaneously pursue stabilization priorities and the strengthening of the health system as a whole without compromising the latter. The key finding from this analysis is that assumptions on what health interventions can contribute to building state legitimacy have already begun to shape policy and programme choices despite the absence of empirical research on both the costs and benefits of health as an instrument of state- or peace-building.

Conclusion

This article has sought to capture the way in which health interventions are perhaps uniquely vulnerable to the pressure for statebuilding outcomes and capture through internal and securitization processes. However, it suggests that the mechanisms through which this has occurred have largely been internal to the health sector rather than through some form of raw and imperial 'securitization' or 'militant liberalism'. Instead of security elites *capturing* and distorting health interventions, this article has suggested that the growing recognition of the impact of conflict on health systems explains the trend towards more holistic approaches to health system strengthening and the greater emphasis placed on 'statebuilding' that characterizes contemporary discourses on health interventions and approaches by donors.

However, whilst Western models of stabilization involve creating a capacity within the host state to govern, and establishing a functioning health service is probably a component of this in many circumstances, the evidential basis is insufficient to determine the relative importance of health interventions in generating state legitimacy when compared with other core activities such as support to security, justice, governance and economic regeneration. Arguably there is a requirement for more systematic research on the nature or natures of state legitimacy, its generation and the interaction between various forms of public service delivery in its creation and maintenance. Eldon *et al.* (2008, p. ix) echo this conclusion but more optimistically suggest that

> health sector strengthening can contribute to state-building in the health sector. It can help build legitimacy and capacity, and put health on the state-building agenda. Context is the key influencer of potential for state-building, but it is often inadequately understood. However, the extent of state-building within the health sector is not systematically understood and more evidence is needed. For instance, there is little, if any, clear evidence on the relationship between health system strengthening, citizen and state expectations and the social compact.

This analysis suggests that there is a requirement for a research agenda which explores empirically the impact that health interventions have on the construction of government legitimacy. However, whilst the evidence of health's contribution to building state legitimacy remains elusive, it is widely agreed in the literature that health planning should continue to reflect the view that whilst statebuilding can be a welcome 'secondary consequence', the primary objective of health provision should remain the enhancement of health outcomes.

Notes on Contributor

Stuart Gordon is a Research Fellow on the Global Health Security and International Security Programmes at Chatham House as well as a lecturer in humanitarianism and development in the Department of International Development at the London School of Economics and Political Science.

Note

1 Interview with Egbert Sondorp, Senior Lecturer in Health and Conflict at the London School of Hygiene and Tropical Medicine, 15 April 2011.

References

Berry, C. et al., 2004a. *Approaches to improving the delivery of social services in difficult environments*. Poverty Reduction in Difficult Environments Team, Policy Division, PRDE working paper 3: DFID.

Berry, C. et al., 2004b. *PRDE working paper 3: approaches to improving the delivery of social services in difficult environments*. London: DFID.

Betsi, N.A., Koudou, B.G., Cissé, G., Tschannen, A.B., Pignol, A.M., Ouattara, Y. et al., 2006. Effect of an armed conflict on human resources and health systems in Côte d'Ivoire: prevention of and care for people with HIV/AIDS. *AIDS Care*, 18 (4), 356–365.

Bornemisza, O. and Zwi, A., 2008. *Neglected health systems research: health policy and systems research in conflict-affected fragile states*. Research Issues, Alliance for Health Policy and Systems Research and the World Health Organization. Available from: http://www.who.int/alliance-hpsr/AllianceHPSR_ResearchIssue_FragileStates.pdf.

Brinkerhoff, D.W., 2008. From humanitarian and post-conflict assistance to health system strengthening in fragile states: clarifying the transition and the role of NGOs. *Health systems 20/20*. Available from: http://www.eldis.org/go/topics/dossiers/health-and-fragile-states/delivering-health-services-in-fragile-states/health-system-strengthening-approaches&id=41999&type=Document.

Cahill, K.M., 1987. A bridge to peace. *Journal of public health policy*, 8 (3), 299–302.

Carlson, C. et al., 2005. *Improving the delivery of health and education services in difficult environments: lessons from case studies*. London: DFID.

Cliff, J. and Noormahomed, A.R., 1988. Health as a target: South Africa's destabilization of Mozambique. *Social science and medicine*, 27 (7), 717–722.

Coghlan, B. et al., 2006. Mortality in the democratic republic of Congo: a nationwide survey. *The Lancet*, 367 (9504), 44–51.

Cometto, G., 2006. Contracting out: a different viewpoint from South Sudan. BMJ 2006, 332:718. Available from: http://www.bmj.com/content/332/7543/718.

Commins, S. and Fenton, W., 2007. *Treading a delicate path: NGOs in fragile states: draft synthesis report*. London: SCF UK.

Coninz, R., 2007. Tuberculosis in complex emergencies. *Bulletin of the World Health Organization*, 85 (8), 569–648.

Cramer, C. and Goodhand, J., 2002. 'Try again. Fail again. Fail better? War, the state and the 'post-conflict' challenge in Afghanistan.' *Development and change*, 33 (5), 885–909.

Department for International Development, 2005. *Why we need to work more effectively in fragile states*. London: DFID. Available from: http://www.jica.go.jp/cdstudy/library/pdf/20071101_11.pdf.

Eldon, J., Hadi, Y. and Waddington, C., 2008. *Health systems reconstruction and state-building*. A paper commissioned by the Health and Fragile States Network. London, HLSP Institute.

Fatimie, A., 2009. Ministry of Public Health Afghanistan. Available from: http://www.moph.gov.af/en/news.php?id=44.

Feldbaum, H. and Michaud, J., 2010. Health diplomacy and the enduring relevance of foreign policy interests. *PLoS medicine*, 7 (4): e1000226. Available from: http://www.plosmedicine.org/article/info:doi%2F10.1371%2Fjournal.pmed.1000226.

Fenton, W., 2007. *Treading a delicate path: NGOs in fragile states. Case study Southern Sudan*. London: Save the Children.

Fidler, P.D., 2005. *Health and foreign policy: a conceptual overview*. London: Nuffield Trust. Available from: http://www.nuffieldtrust.org.uk/ecomm/files/040205Fidler.pdf.

Fritz, V. and Menocal, A.R., 2008. *Understanding state-building from a political economy perspective: an analytical and conceptual paper on processes, embedded tensions and lessons for international engagement*. London: ODI.

Gele, A.A. and Bjune, G., 2010. Armed conflicts have an impact on the spread of tuberculosis: the case of the Somali Regional State of Ethiopia. *Conflict and health*, 4 (1), 4–1.

Gordon, S., 2010. *Winning hearts and minds*. Feinstein Centre. Available from: http://www.humansecuritygateway.com/documents/FIC-Winning-Hearts-Minds-Aid-Security-Helmand.pdf.

Gordon, S., 2011a. Health, stabilization and securitization: towards understanding the drivers of the military role in health interventions. *Medicine, conflict and survival*, 27 (1), 43–66.

Gordon, S., 2011b. *Helmand and stabilisation, 2006–2008*. Boston, MA: Feinstein Center, Tufts University.

Guerra de Macedo, C., 1994. Health, development and peacemaking: Health as a bridge for peace. Speech made at the international symposium on Health, Development, Conflict Resolution and Peacemaking, 3 June, Copenhagen, Denmark. Copenhagen: World Health Organization.

Gunn, S., 2009. Health as a bridge to peace. *Canadian medical association journal*, 180 (12), 34.

Gutlove, P., 1997. Health bridges for peace: integrating health care and community reconciliation. *Medicine, conflict and survival*, 14, 6–23.

Hansen, P.M. and Peters, D.H., 2008. Measuring and managing progress in the establishment of basic health services: the Afghanistan health sector balanced scorecard. *International journal of health planning management*, 23 (2), 107–117.

Harris, S., 2004. Marrying foreign policy and health: feasible or doomed to fail? *Medical journal of Australia*, 180, 171–173. Available from: http://www.mja.com.au/public/issues/180_04_160204/har10834_fm.html.

Hess, G. and Pfeiffer, M., 1999. *Comparative analysis of WHO 'Health as a bridge for peace' case studies*. Geneva: World Health Organization. Available from: http://www.who.int/hac/techniguidance/hbp/comparative_analysis/en/print/html.

Horton, R., 2007. Health as an instrument of foreign policy. *Lancet*, 369, 806–807.

Jones, S.G., ed., 2006. *Securing health: lessons from nation-building missions*. Santa Monica, CA: RAND Corporation. Available from: http://www.rand.org/pubs/monographs/2006/RAND_MG321.pdf.

Jones, B. et al., 2008. *From fragility to resilience: concepts and dilemmas of state-building in fragile states*. Research paper for the Fragile States Group of the Development Assistance Committee of the Organisation for Economic Co-operation and Development (OECD DAC). Paris: OECD DAC. Available from: http://www.cic.nyu.edu/global/docs/fragilitytoresilience.pdf.

Keane, V., 1996. *Health impact of large post-conflict migratory movements: the experience of Mozambique*. Geneva: International Organization for Migration.

Killcullen, D., 2005. *28 articles of counterinsurgency*. Available from: http://www.d-n-i.net/fcs/pdf/kilcullen_28_articles.pdf.

Krug, M.E. and Freedman, L.P., 2008. Assessing health system performance in developing countries: a review of the literature. *Health policy*, 85 (3), 263–276.

Krug, E. et al., 2002. The world report on violence and health. *The Lancet*, 360 (9339), 1083–1088.

Lancet, 2005. Editorial: A crucial time for Afghanistan's fledgling health system. *The Lancet*, 365, 819–820.

Laurence, C. and Poole, L., 2005. *Service delivery in difficult environments: transferable approaches from the humanitarian community*. A report for Merlin. Author's copy,

Leader, N. and Colenso, P., 2005. *Aid instruments in fragile states*. PRDE Working Paper 5—Poverty Reduction in Difficult Environments Team/Aid Effectiveness Team Policy Division. London: DFID.

Levy, B. and Sidel, V., eds, 2008. *War and public health*. New York and Oxford: Oxford University Press.

Loevinsohn, B. and Harding, A., 2005. Buying results? Contracting for health service delivery in developing countries. *The Lancet*, 366, 676–681.

Loevinsohn, B. and Sayed, G.D., 2008. Lessons from the health sector in Afghanistan: how progress can be made in challenging circumstances. *Journal of the American Medical Association*, 300 (6), 724–726.

MacQueen, G., McCutcheon, G. and Santa-Barbara, J., 1997. The use of health initiatives as peace initiatives. *Peace and change*, 22 (2), 175–197.

Macrae, J. and Harmer, A., 2004. Beyond the continuum: and overview of the changing role of aid policy in protracted crises. In: J. Macrae and A. Harmer, eds. HPG report 18, *Beyond the continuum, the changing role of aid in protracted crises*. London: ODI.

Macrae, J. and Leader, N., 2000. *The politics of coherence: humanitarianism and foreign policy in the post-Cold War era*. London: Overseas Development Institute. Available from: http://www.odi.org.uk/hpg/papers/researchinfocus1.pdf.

Marine Corps, 2007. *The US Army/Marine Corps counterinsurgency field manual: US Army field manual no. 3-24: Marine Corps warfighting publication no. 3-33.5*. Chicago: University of Chicago Press.

McInnes, C. and Lee, K., 2006. Health, security and foreign policy. *Review of international studies*, 32 (1), 5–23.

Menocal, A.R., 2009. *State-building for peace: navigating an arena of contradictions*. London: ODI.

MOD, 2010. *UK MOD, Security and stabilisation: the military contribution.* Available from: http://www.mod.uk/NR/rdonlyres/C403A6C7-E72C-445E-8246-D11002D7A852/0/20091201jdp_40UDCDCIMAPPS.pdf.

Nagai, M. et al., 2007. Reconstruction of health service systems in the post-conflict northern province in Sri Lanka. *Health policy*, 83 (1), 84–93.

Newbrander, W., 2007. *Rebuilding health systems and providing health services in fragile states. Management sciences for health.* Occasional Paper no. 7. USAID. Available from: http://www.msh.org/Documents/OccasionalPapers/upload/Rebuilding-Health-Systems-and-Providing-Health-Services-in-Fragile-States.pdf.

Newbrander, W., Yoder, R. and Debevoise, A.B., 2007. Rebuilding health systems in post-conflict countries: estimating the costs of basic services. *International journal of health planning and management*, 2 (4), 319–336.

Nye, J., 2002. One world: health turns into a security priority. *International Herald Tribune*, 2 September.

Overseas Development Institute (ODI), 2003. Rebuilding health services after conflict: lessons from East Timor and Afghanistan. London: ODI. Available from: http://www.reliefweb.int/rw/rwb.nsf/AllDocsByUNID/728dcebad50f486085256dd5006fd68a15.

Owen, J. and Roberts, O., 2005. Globalization, health and foreign policy: emerging linkages and interests. *Global health*, 1 (12). Available from: http://www.globalizationandhealth.com/contenet/1/1/12.

Palmer, N. and Strong, L., 2006. Health policy—contracting out health services in fragile states. *British medical journal*, 332 (7543), 718–721.

Palmer, N. et al., 2005. Health policy in Afghanistan: two years of rapid change. London: London School of Hygiene and Tropical Medicine. Author's copy.

Panter-Brick, C., 2010. Conflict, violence, and health: setting a new interdisciplinary agenda. *Social science and medicine*, 70 (1), 1–6.

Pavanello, S. and Darcy, J., 2008. *Improving the provision of basic services for the poor in fragile environments: international literature review synthesis paper.* London: ODI. Available from: http://www.gsdrc.org/go/display&type=Document&id=3331.

Pavignani, E., 2005. *Health service delivery in post-conflict states.* Available from: http://www.hlfhealthmdgs.org/Documents/HealthServiceDelivery.pdf.

Pavignani, E. and Colombo, A., 2001. *Providing health services in countries disrupted by civil wars: a comparative analysis of Mozambique and Angola, 1975–2000.* Geneva: WHO, Department of Emergency and Humanitarian Action.

Pedersen, D., 2002. Political violence, ethnic conflict, and contemporary wars: broad implications for health and social well-being. *Social science and medicine*, 55 (2), 175–190.

Peters, D. et al., 2007. A balanced scorecard for health services in Afghanistan. *Bulletin of the World Health Organization*, 85 (2), 146–151.

Ponsar, F. et al., 2009. Mortality, violence and access to care in two districts of Port-au-Prince, Haiti. *Conflict and health*, 3 (4).

Roberts, B., Guy, S., Sondorp, E. and Lee-Jones, L. 2008. A basic package of health services for post-conflict countries: implications for sexual and reproductive health services. *Reproductive health matters*, 16 (31), 57–64.

Rodriguez-Garcia, R., Schlesser, M. and Bernstein, R., 2001. *How can health serve as a bridge to peace?* Washington, DC: George Washington University/USAID/CERTI. Available from: http://www.certi.org/publications/policy/gwc-12a-brief.PDF.

Rubenstein, L., 2009. *Post-conflict health reconstruction: new foundations for U.S. policy.* Washington: United States Institute of Peace. Available from: http://www.usip.org/files/post-conflict_health_reconstruction.pdf.

Rushton, S. and McInnes, C., 2006. The UK, health and peace-building: the mysterious disappearance of health as a bridge for peace. *Medicine, conflict and survival*, 22 (2), 94–109.

Sabri, B. et al., 2007. Towards sustainable delivery of health services in Afghanistan: options for the future. *Bulletin of the World Health Organization*, 85, 712–718.

Santa Barbara, J. and MacQueen, G., 2004. Peace through health: key concepts. *The Lancet*, 364 (9431), 384–386.

Thieren, M., 2007. Health and foreign policy in question: the case of humanitarian action. *Bulletin of the World Health Organization*, 85 (3), 218–224.

Tiwari, S. et al., 2005. Prevalence of TB and service utilization in conflict affected areas of Nepal. *Journal of Nepal Health Research Council*, 3 (1), 45–57.

United States Department of State, 2009. *United States government counterinsurgency guide*. Available from: http://www.state.gov/documents/organization/119629.pdf.

USAID, 2005. *Fragile states strategy*. Available from: http://pdf.usaid.gov/pdf_docs/PDACA999.pdf.

Utzinger, J. and Weiss, M., 2007. Editorial: Armed conflict, war and public health. *Tropical medicine and international health*, 12, 903–906.

Vass, A., 2001. Peace through health. *British medical journal*, 323 (7320), 10–20.

Vergeer, P., Canavan, A. and Rothmann, I., 2009. *A rethink on the use of aid mechanisms in health sector early recovery*. Amsterdam: Development Policy and Practice. Available from: http://www.kit.nl/net/KIT_Publicaties_output/ShowFile2.aspx?e=1508.

Waldman, R., 2003. *Rebuilding health services after conflict: lessons learnt from East Timor and Afghanistan*. London: ODI. Available from: http://www.odihpn.org/report.asp?id=2567.

Waldman, R., 2006. *Health programming in post-conflict fragile states*. Basic Support for Institutionalizing Child Survival (BASICS) for the United States Agency for International Development (USAID). Available from: http://www.msh.org/Documents/Occasional Papers/upload/Rebuilding-Health-Systems-and-Providing-Health-Services-in-Fragile-States.pdf.

Waldman, R., 2007. *Health programming for rebuilding states: a briefing paper*. Arlington, VA: Basic Support for Institutionalizing Child Survival (BASICS) for US Agency for International Development.

Waldman, R., Strong, L. and Wali, A., 2006. *Afghanistan's health system since 2001: condition improved, prognosis cautiously optimistic*. Afghanistan Research and Evaluation Unit, Kabul. Available from: http://www.reliefweb.int/rw/RWFiles2006.nsf/FilesByRWDocUnidFilename/KHII-72J7PB-full_report.pdf/$File/full_report.pdf.

Whaites, A., 2009. *States in development: understanding state-building. Working paper*. London: DFID, 2009.

Wheeler, V., Graces, S. and Wesley, M., 2006. *From crisis-response to state-building: services and stability in conflict-affected contexts*. London: ODI. Available from: http://www.odi.org.uk/resources/hpg-publications/commissioned-reports/2006/crisis-response-statebuilding-services-stability-conflict.pdf.

Wilder, A., 2010. Aid and stability in Pakisatan: lessons from the 2005 earthquake response. *Disasters special issue: states of fragility: stabilisation and its implications for humanitarian action*, 34 (s3), s406–s426.

World Health Organization (WHO), 2002. *World report on violence and health*. Geneva: World Health Organization.

World Health Organization (WHO), 2005. *Guide to health workforce development in post-conflict environments*. Available from: http://whqlibdoc.who.int/publications/2005/9241593288_eng.pdf.

World Health Organization (WHO), 2006. *What is Health as a Bridge for Peace*. WHO Health as a Bridge for Peace Project. Geneva: World Health Organization. Available from: http://www.who.int/hac/techguidance/hbp/about/en/print.html.

World Bank, 2004. World Development Report: making services work for the poor. World Bank. Available from: http://www.who.int/entity/trade/events/UNGA_RESOLUTION_GHFP_63_33.pdf.

Zivetz, L., 2006. *Health service delivery in early recovery fragile states: lessons from Afghanistan, Cambodia, Mozambique and Timor Leste*. Arlington, VA: Basic Support for Institutionalizing Child Survival (BASICS) for the United States/Agency for International Development. Available from: http://www.basics.org/documents/Early_Recovery_Fragile_States_Zivetz_Final.pdf.

Zwi, A., 1991. Militarism, militarization, health and the third world. *Medicine and war*, 7, 262–268.

Zwi, A., Ugalde, A. and Richards, P., 2008. The effects of war and political violence on health services. *In*: L. Kurtz, ed. *Encyclopedia of violence, peace and conflict*. San Diego, CA: Academic Press, 933–943.

An Empirical Approach to Post-conflict Legitimacy: Victims' Needs and the Everyday

Simon Robins

An empirical study has been made of victims of conflict in Timor-Leste and Nepal seeking a qualitative understanding of local post-conflict priorities. It allows an appreciation to emerge of how the conflict-affected conceive of legitimacy and quality of governance, with victims emphasizing basic needs, an addressing of issues of marginalization and the incorporation of indigenous understandings of the meaning of peace. The data in this study motivate a victim-centred discussion of both the limitations of liberal approaches to peace and the implications for the legitimacy of post-conflict governance of prioritizing the everyday needs of the conflict-affected, in contrast to universal and institutionally rooted liberal values.

Post-conflict societies are defined as such by the histories of violence they have experienced and which are inscribed in the minds and on the bodies of their victims. This study aims to understand the implications of those histories and of the presence of victims for the legitimacy of post-conflict governance, by investigating victims' priorities for a post-conflict peace. Liberal approaches attempt to address legacies of violence through the discourses of human rights and transitional justice (Paris 2004), rather than through reference to the needs and priorities of those most affected by such violence. The liberal peace, characterized by a commitment to a set of values that are presented as universal, but that emerge from the assumptions of Western liberal democracy, ignores the local and the particular of both peace and conflict, and subordinates indigenous perspectives and traditional culture to a prescriptive technical and procedural approach (Richmond 2009a). The rights discourse exemplifies this, offering a set of institutions, including trials and truth commissions, which can be 'rolled out' according to international precedent in any context (Teitel 2000, Hayner 2011). Here, the everyday needs of victims of conflict will be understood, situated in the social and symbolic worlds in which they live, and the implications for legitimacy of governance in their communities discussed.

The article begins by discussing understandings of legitimacy, dominated by approaches that focus on global benchmarks, and reviews how mechanisms of the liberal peace construct victims in narrow and universalized terms. The contexts of Nepal and Timor-Leste, and the ethnographic methodology of the study, are introduced and the results of an assessment of victims' needs presented. These data are then used to critique liberal and universalist approaches to legitimacy, in favour of a contextualized approach, driven by local and particular everyday lives and needs of post-conflict populations.

Post-conflict Legitimacy and the Everyday

Legitimacy of governance refers to the acceptance by populations of a regime as correct and appropriate (Brinkerhoff 2005), ultimately understood to revolve around a population's willingness to be ruled: 'A state's (or government's) legitimacy is the complex moral right it possesses to be the exclusive imposer of binding duties on its subjects, to have its subjects comply with these duties, and to use coercion to enforce the duties' (Simmons 2001, p. 130). This definition, however, says little about what constitutes legitimacy, emphasizing that it is largely the product of the consent of the ruled. Post-conflict legitimacy has traditionally been perceived as emerging from normative models of governance, and a consequence of the hegemony of liberal approaches is that legitimacy of governance in states emerging from conflict is measured in terms of global benchmarks, focussing on institutional state-based measures and alienated from the lives and needs of populations. The liberal peace has defined 'good governance' as dependent upon liberalization, democracy and human rights (e.g. de Alcantara 1998, Brinkerhoff 2007). In states emerging from a violent past, the rights discourse drives institutional approaches to victims of violence and the addressing of conflict-era violations through prioritizing truth and accountability, widely perceived to restore the rule of law and boost legitimacy (e.g. Kritz 1996). The mechanisms of trials and truth commissions are emblematic of the proceduralism of liberal approaches to legitimacy, driven by an external universalism which is norm-based and prescriptive. Truth commissions have been described as 'one of the main ways in which a bureaucratic elite seeks to manufacture legitimacy for state institutions' (Wilson 2001, p. 19), fetishizing victims and their testimony, but ultimately existing to legitimate the new state rather than benefit victims (Humphrey 2002). There are few studies that attempt to empirically understand the impact of such mechanisms on post-conflict legitimacy from the perspective of the citizens upon whose consent to rule legitimacy depends.

Whilst addressing the needs of the population does not figure highly in the governance literature in comparison with the satisfaction of international norms, there is an emerging literature that challenges such norms as the sole basis for the legitimacy of governance. Milliken and Krause (2002), for example, suggest that the addressing of everyday needs is a source of legitimacy for the state, expanding understandings of what creates conditions for governance from security and order to welfare and basic needs. Given that the populations of post-conflict states are often characterized by their extreme and unmet needs, the effectiveness of a state in delivering core services and addressing needs is perceived as impacting upon its legitimacy (Clapham 2003, Call and Cousens 2008). Defining legitimacy locally, rather than according to global benchmarks, and understanding that populations legitimate states according to the lives they lead, has been called 'performance legitimacy' (Francois and Sud 2006), relating both to the policy priorities made and the quality of their realization. A liberal peace that perceives legitimacy as constructed in metropolitan institutions rather than in the communities where people live can be irrelevant to such local priorities and thus struggle to be perceived as legitimate.

The empirical studies discussed here offer an alternative to universal and norm-based understandings of legitimacy: an evidence-based approach, where the priorities of those most impacted by conflict are understood in the context of the communities in which the social meanings that underpin legitimacy are constructed. Rather than examining the institutions of the state, such an approach studies popular perceptions of them. This kind of methodology is necessarily context dependent, abandoning the idea that there exists a set of liberal criteria that are universally valid in favour of an appreciation that both between and within states, perceptions of legitimacy can vary widely. It also implies not a technocratic, metropolitan-led approach, but one rooted in the everyday lives and experiences of populations emerging from conflict, and this drives the victim-centred approach taken here. The methodologies of such empirical work have largely been considered irrelevant to the international relations milieu from which most discussion of legitimacy originates, but tools such as the ethnographic methods discussed here can both inform and challenge norm-based understandings by allowing the voices of those who determine legitimacy to emerge. The relative priority assigned by populations to performance legitimacy (i.e. satisfaction of needs-based demands of the state) and to regime legitimacy (those elements that are norm-based and relate to institutions and formal structures of governance) can be evaluated using such methods.

The focus on victims of conflict emerges as a result of the fact that their presence exemplifies the impact of conflict and plays an important role in perceptions of legitimacy and in community attitudes to the post-conflict dispensation. Despite this, however, victims are largely absent from efforts to understand legitimacy. Often the locus of a spoiler problem will be a victim community seeking recognition of and redress for a grievance (Stedman 1997): the perceived suffering of victims will serve to mobilize a community and legitimate a discourse of continued violence, while delegitimating the authorities. This is particularly true in traditional societies where networks of social relations provoke much stronger obligations than are felt to the state (Boege *et al.* 2009). Post-conflict legitimacy is constituted from the collective meanings assigned to the conflict and to the peace, and from community perceptions of the state and their rulers. To gain an empirical grasp of the concept of legitimacy demands that the grievances of victims be understood as broadly as they are by their communities, and not according to some external and prescriptive discourse. Victim-centred approaches (Robins 2011) can act as a test of the perceived quality of governance at the grassroots, using a sample of those most affected by conflict. Conflict victims are the most vulnerable in their communities; they are, for example, the displaced, the disabled, the orphaned and the widowed: they are visible to their community as in need of services from the state and represent the greatest challenge to the *effectiveness* of the state: as such they represent a substantial test of performance legitimacy.

Conflict Victims as Subjects of the Liberal Peace

Liberal interventions after conflict typically consider the state as their principal frame of reference, and a significant driver of liberal peace interventions is the global (and state-centred) discourse of rights, which emphasizes a perpetrator and violation-centred approach to legacies of violence. This has led to a focus on judicial process and 'truth-telling' bodies as an intrinsic part of peacebuilding: whilst victims are the principal performers in such mechanisms they operate in urban spaces in the capital, remote from the lives of rural victims. Such approaches neglect the fact that the most extreme impacts of violence are felt at the human level and so efforts to address their legacy must also unfold on a scale far below that of the institutions of the state.

Normatively driven rights-based approaches ensure that the institutions of peacebuilding are steered by experts remote from communities most affected by violations: the subjects of liberalism are constructed on a basis with little resonance with local norms. The discourse of rights, as one of the ideological planks of liberal peacebuilding, serves to ensure that agency lies with elites in the capital rather than ordinary people (Robins 2010a, Richmond 2010). In a state where only elites 'know' what rights are, they necessarily become something that are largely claimed *on behalf of* victims rather than by victims themselves, substituting passivity for empowerment and dependence upon others (Madlingozi 2010).[1] Whilst the rights discourse claims to address all rights equally, in practice civil and political rights are prioritized over others, notably the social, economic and cultural (Arbour 2007, Richmond 2010, Roberts 2011), particularly after conflict. Thus, rights come with their own priorities, which serve to depoliticize the discussion of peacebuilding, marginalizing agendas of social and economic justice in favour of a legalism that privileges the civil and political, i.e. regime legitimacy over performance legitimacy. Needs, in contrast, are the natural articulation of perceived deficits that arise in victims' everyday lives, comprising both direct impacts of the violation to which they were subject and those which emerge from the context of poverty and marginalization that characterize states in conflict. Needs are subjective, local and contingent, situated in and of the highly social worlds people occupy.

The Two Case Studies

The two case studies represent one state, Nepal, where liberal peacebuilding has yet to unfold on any scale, and one, Timor-Leste, where such processes are considered largely complete, despite their manifest failure. Both are states with dispersed rural and agricultural populations of great ethnic diversity emerging from conflicts driven by alienation from their rulers. At the time of the research they had almost identical per capita GDP,[2] representing some of the poorest states in Asia.

Timor-Leste emerged from centuries of Portuguese colonial rule and 25 years of brutal Indonesian occupation to be subject to the full machinery of liberal peacebuilding. From October 1999 Timor-Leste was governed under UN trusteeship, and the state was considered a blank slate upon which liberal prescriptions could be inscribed (Richmond and Franks 2008). In terms of addressing the massive violations of the Indonesian period, a UN-led serious crimes process (ICTJ 2006) and a truth commission, the Comissão de Acolhimento, Verdade e Reconciliação de Timor Leste (CAVR, Commission for Welcome, Truth and Reconciliation) (CAVR 2005) were created by a UN administration. The serious crimes process, focussed almost exclusively on the violence around Indonesia's departure in 1999, reflected the international community's preoccupation with accountability, while the Timorese leadership spoke against this and in favour of reconciliation: 'We have to see what we can do, not what we wish to do. Now we need reconciliation and we have to think of socio-economic rather than formal justice. That is our priority' (Xanana Gusmão, while President, 16 December 2005). CAVR's much lauded engagement with tradition revolved around the use of traditional local dispute resolution techniques, to reconcile perpetrators of less serious offences to their communities, in the Community Reconciliation Process (CRP) (Babo-Soares 2004, Ximenes 2004, Kent 2005). Some of the only literature on CAVR that comes from Timorese who did not work with the Commission is from *La'o Hamutuk*, a Timorese NGO (La'o Hamutuk 2003) and perhaps the only source that clearly states the CAVR model of truth and reconciliation as foreign in origin: 'many key staff, all funding, and the basic structure and methodology come from overseas.... it has relied heavily on international consultants, advisors, and leadership' (ibid., p. 1). Despite the cooption of elements of indigenous process in the CRP, the basic philosophy of the Commission regarding the therapeutic value of truth as healing, for both individuals and the nation, was imported from global discourses, notably that emerging from the South African Truth and Reconciliation Commission. Less present in the literature is the 'valorization' programme that has led to tens of thousands of veterans of the liberation struggle, both military and civilian, receiving medals since late 2006 (World Bank 2008), and others receiving pensions and economic support: it is the mechanism referencing Timor's violent past that has directly affected the greatest number of Timorese. The independence of Timor-Leste was formalized in 2002, only for the state to descend into chaos in 2006, with police and military exchanging gunfire on the streets of Dili against a background of ethnically driven violence (UN 2006), provoking both the return of UN-sponsored troops and more serious reflection on a peacebuilding and statebuilding intervention that had until then been considered a great success by those leading it.

Timor-Leste's population stands at a little over 1 million (Government of Timor-Leste 2010): 72 per cent of these live in rural areas, working largely in subsistence agriculture, and 37 per cent have an income below $1.25 per day (World Bank 2010). In addition to widespread poverty, the legacy of the nation's violent past remains, with estimates that as many as one-third of Timor-Leste's population died as a result of the Indonesian invasion (Staveteig 2007), many of their bodies never having been found. Whilst 90 per cent of East Timorese claim to be Catholic, almost all continue to hold traditional beliefs; the structure of local secular and sacred hierarchies and the network of obligations between and within families creates a unified structure that traditionally represented both local governance and law (Hohe and Nixon 2001). In this sense, understandings of both governance and justice are 'socio-cosmic' (ibid., p. 11), deeply embedded in kinship and in shared beliefs of spiritual understandings arising from the importance of acting in accordance with the wishes of the ancestors.

The second set of data comes from Nepal. Nepal is the poorest country in Asia: 55 per cent of the population lives on less than $1.25 per day (World Bank 2010). The feudal social relations that have persisted into modern times impact upon livelihoods, with a significant proportion of the rural population lacking access to land: 10 per cent of the rural population is absolutely landless and 58 per cent functionally landless, with holdings too small for subsistence (Uprety et al. 2005). A lack of access to land is the dominant cause of rural poverty. Nepal is a mosaic of ethnicities, languages and castes, unified in the eighteenth century under a high-caste dynasty that migrated from India in the centuries before. The many other ethnicities in Nepal, notably the indigenous who have traditional animistic and Buddhist beliefs and the lower castes, have been systematically excluded from the very idea of the Nepali nation (Höfer 1979, Hachhethu 2003, Tiwari 2007). At the start of the twenty-first century the Brahmin and Chhetri castes, which constitute some 30 per cent of the population of Nepal, made up 87 per cent of civil service staff (Battachan 2006), with clear implications for representation and legitimacy. Nepal's conflict was driven by poverty and social exclusion: following democratization in 1990, a Marxist party, the Communist Party of Nepal (Maoist) (CPN-M), declared a 'People's War' against the regime in 1996 (Ogura 2008). The conflict escalated to the point where the Maoists had effective control of much of the territory of the state, including almost all rural areas. The decade-long conflict ended in 2006 when constitutional parties united with the Maoists to overthrow a king who had seized absolute power. A legacy of the conflict was a death toll of 16,000, largely at the hands of the state (INSEC 2007), with thousands more disappeared (ICRC 2008). Nepal's transition remains incomplete, with political paralysis characterizing the situation since the CPN-M became the largest party in the legislature, following elections in 2008. A UN mission to Nepal, with a limited mandate to monitor the arms and armies of the parties to the conflict, has left the country and liberal peacebuilding remains frustrated by the lack of a stable polity.

Methodology

Methods to understand people's needs and the evidence of everyday lives must be able to operate within the realm of local ontologies, challenging liberal universalism. This privileges ethnographic methodologies, which confront the 'thin' legalistic representations of liberal discourses with 'thick description' (Geertz 1977). This also permits a challenging of the universalizing effect of the theory which dominates discussions of both peacebuilding and legitimacy, including those advocating emancipatory approaches.

These studies (Robins 2009, 2010b) aimed to use qualitative research methods with a sample of victims of serious violations occurring during the conflicts in Nepal and Timor-Leste to understand their needs. The sampling frames used were lists of persons missing[3] as a result of the conflicts and collected by the International Committee of the Red Cross (ICRC 2003). These included persons killed but whose bodies had not been retrieved, those missing following arrest by a party to the conflict, and those who had become separated from families and not seen again, notably in Timor when populations were fleeing in the mountains. This data-set was the result of families of the missing visiting ICRC offices and of ICRC delegates meeting families in all areas of the country over the entire periods of conflict. Whilst this sampling frame contains only victims of certain violations, they are violations that have come to characterize both conflicts and have been identified and recorded by credible sources

A selection was made of four of Timor-Leste's 13 districts, and ten of Nepal's 72, including those most affected by violence, and within these districts cases were selected at random from the ICRC list and the families of victims visited in their homes. In Timor-Leste, a total of 69 families were interviewed and 81 relatives of victims met in nine focus groups, and in Nepal 86 families were interviewed and 74 relatives met in ten focus groups. Focus groups were organized by victims' organizations and (in Timor) by local community leaders. Families of the dead and the missing were interviewed using a semi-structured approach driven by a qualitative questionnaire that had been developed iteratively through contact with victims and victims' groups. The aim was to understand families' broad needs arising from their experience of conflict and their expectations of the authorities. Families were asked what needs they saw as emerging from their victimhood and, in Timor-Leste, their opinion of the mechanisms to address violations, namely trials, CAVR and the valorization processes. Interviews were recorded, translated and transcribed and these transcriptions constitute the raw data of the study.

Towards an Empirically Guided Post-conflict Peacebuilding

In principle, a victim is defined as such by what has been done to him or her, with this codified in the violations defined by various bodies of law. In practice, victimhood does not emerge naturally from the experience of being harmed, but is constructed socially and subjectively, with a range of factors determining who will be accorded victim status. Most formally, bodies established to deal with victims, such as Truth Commissions or prosecutorial bodies, will determine who is considered a victim. More locally, in many contexts victims' groups and NGOs will engage with victims and define criteria that may impact on understandings of victimhood within communities. These understandings may or may not coincide with those of victims themselves, usually being created by those with authority in the capital and remote from affected communities. A political agenda or a certain narrative of the conflict may privilege a particular conception of victimhood: victims constitute a part of the contested terrain of the memory of the conflict, at both national and local levels, creating a hierarchy of victimhood (Rombouts 2002). The Truth Commission represents the formalization of this process, in which victim memory is transformed into public knowledge (Humphrey 2002), sanctioned by authority. Victims were selected for this study on the basis of having a relative missing in the conflict, largely on their own understanding. However, since victims' associations played a key role in contact with victim families, these understandings were in most cases shared by their communities.

The needs and priorities of victims of conflict are summarized as they emerged in the study, with the aim of understanding implications for post-conflict legitimacy. Whilst human rights advocates seek to frame responses to violations in terms of rights, it has been seen in both Timor and Nepal that most victims, dominated as they are by the rural, poor and illiterate, know little or nothing of rights and articulate *needs*, often urgent needs with which they are confronted on a daily basis. This view is exemplified in the comment of the sister-in-law of a man disappeared by the state, in Rolpa, Nepal:

> We hear people on the radio talking about these things. But nobody has come and told us about our rights. We don't have any concept of human rights. (Kotgaun, Rolpa, 11 June 2008)

Needs of Victims

The priorities of victim families emerged from an initial open question, with dominant needs being those for economic support, truth about the fate and

Table 1. Needs expressed by families of the missing

	Families expressing this need, %	
Need	Timor-Leste	Nepal
Economic support	61	62
Truth about fate / access to body	46	64
Prosecution	10	29

Source: Robins (2009).

access to the body of the missing. Recognition, in terms of an acknowledgment from the authorities of what had happened, was also a priority, particularly in Timor-Leste, where 30 per cent mentioned it as a priority (Robins 2009).

There is a significant difference in needs expressed by families in the capitals and those in rural areas: almost 3 times as many families outside Dili as in the capital prioritized economic needs, while 10 times as many in Kathmandu expressed a need for prosecutions as in the rural district of Bardiya, populated largely by indigenous Tharu (Robins 2009, 2010b). The data demonstrate that even within a state needs are highly local, being strongly mediated by economic circumstance, education and degree of marginalization. The need expressed by the greatest number of families was for economic support; many families having lost breadwinners are confronted with the daily struggle to find the money to send children to school, to feed their families, and to pay for expensive rituals for the dead of the conflict. Victims living in poverty share the needs of all the poor and confirm the need for a positive peace that emphasizes livelihood. Such a peace also entails not a return to the structural violence of the past but a transformative process that challenges the violence of many social relations and the social exclusion seen for example by the indigenous people of Nepal. State legitimacy will come not from inclusion or development initiatives in the capital, but effective access to services and livelihood in the rural areas where most live.

In both Nepal and Timor, the understanding that a missing loved one is dead has often come as a result of the time they have been missing or as a result of contact with the spirit, in dreams or otherwise, that is perceived as confirming death. The most important cultural element of the expressed needs was the performance of rituals that would permit the spirits of the dead to rest in peace, and this was emphasized in Timor where the consequences of not performing rituals for the dead were believed to be the potential sickness and death of family members, and instances of both were reported during interviews. For example, the brother of one missing man from Bobonaro stated that:

> [the spirits] take over the place and we cannot keep any animals because many died and only a few of us were left alive. For this reason we always get sick, we cannot domesticate our animals properly and we cannot live in peace, because the spirits are too strong. [...] [They are the spirits of] those who died without knowing where they are buried. [...] You know, us Timorese, how we deal with

> the spirits. We know they died, but just think we did not get to bury them, and they died disgracefully, because we were not able to do any rituals; that is why they always come to disturb our family. (Los Palos, 13 August 2009)

For Timorese families a malign spirit is the most negative potential impact of a missing relative; addressing the issue of those who died in the conflict means not only addressing the needs of their families but also the demands of the spirits. For some families interviewed the peace of the nation is dependent upon this, with recent violence perceived as arising from the many spirits of the conflict dead still not at rest. The father of a missing man in Dili said:

> If the authorities do not do anything to address [the issue of the spirits of the dead], many people will suffer again, because I believe that something else might happen: like a tragedy for the Nation. Let us face it, in 2006 what happened? In 2008, the 11th of February the President was shot ... and for those of us who believe in the spirits, the understanding was that this land is holy or sacred. So all I am asking for the authorities to follow up quickly in order to stop any other tragedy happening to this country. [...] Still they take no action. I have told them, for whoever rules this nation, if we have done nothing for them [the spirits], they will always shake up this country. (Colmera, Dili, 13 July 2009)

The normatively driven global emphasis on accountability is not shared by victims for whom law emerges from traditional dispute resolution and has little to do with the central institutions of the state. When asked explicitly about the need for prosecutions, only a minority in Timor sought them, and in Nepal a bare majority understand justice as meaning prosecutions. Justice was seen rather as receiving compensation or other acknowledgement from the state, or an answer about the fate of the missing. Similarly, a need for reconciliation which has driven the truth commission as a response to violent pasts, or needs linked to problems with or between communities, were articulated by no one interviewed. The overwhelming priority among typical rural victims was for their livelihood, to see the everyday poverty in which most live, and that has been worsened by the loss of relatives, addressed. Since almost all the missing are men, most of those left behind are women, who face challenges arising from the patriarchal structure of their societies and dominant attitudes within them. Both family and community resent the fact that wives do not dress or behave as expected of widows, since many refuse to accept their husbands are dead. Issues over their identity in a society where women's roles are narrowly defined are problematic, with the wives of the missing subject to discrimination and gossip. This demonstrates how the impact of violations arises from the nature of the societies in which victims live and drives women's demands that approaches to the violence of the past must also seek to transform the social hierarchies that increase its impact.

Recognition and acknowledgement was also important to many, particularly in Timor: when explicitly asked, 69 per cent of families sought a memorial to the missing and the dead, particularly important where there is no body. Constructions of national and local memory become crucial to permit victims' families to believe that the sacrifice of the dead and missing are valued; these contribute to a political economy of memory that can be used to legitimate or delegitimate post-conflict regimes. Sources of greatest resistance to the current dispensation in Timor are veterans of the resistance who feel both they and their dead comrades have been forgotten by those now in power; in Nepal, Maoists continue to use narratives of the sacrifice of the 'martyrs' of the war to rally support for ongoing political struggles against the political status quo. The study revealed the extent to which attitudes to the political leadership in both states have been shaped by feelings that victims and those who fought for freedom have been betrayed, and the potential implications of this:

> Our leaders should pay attention, we don't point our finger at the people who killed our father, but we only pass our message to the leaders to pay more attention to the orphans and widows whose loved ones are dead or missing during the war. (Relative of three people killed in internal Fretilin fighting, Manatuto, Timor-Leste, 22 July 2009)

> Even though I lack those things I will never beg, you know. Why do you wait so long to give some subsidy, do you think we don't deserve it? Listen here, with that long time waiting I remind you that it could lead to another conflict because you're not taking care of our situation. (Disabled mother of missing man, Dili, Timor-Leste, 13 September 2009)

In Nepal, at a time when the CPN-M was in government, victims whose loved ones had died in the People's War stated that, if their needs were not addressed, a majority would react: half would take part in a political movement, while a significant minority (15 per cent) say they would be prepared to launch a rebellion with the use of arms, even against their own party:

> The government has to understand our grievances and it has to respect our dignity. If the government of this twenty first century does not understand our problem, the counter-revolution will take place. (Brother of disappeared man, Gorkha, 16 June 2008)

Given that many of these families are cadres of the Maoist party, the implications for the future of the peace process of ignoring the needs of such victims should not be under-estimated. For such potential spoilers to accept the legitimacy of the regime they seek both memorialization of the dead and economic support of the living.

Contrasting Local Needs with Liberal Prescription

In Timor the needs of victims can be compared with the mechanisms put in place as part of peacebuilding efforts, particularly those intended to address issues of violations. The dominant attitude of most families of victims is one of ignorance: hardly any families knew of the limited judicial processes that had taken place, and no family was met whose case had been heard by any court. Similarly, few victim families knew of CAVR or had contact with the Commission: 11 per cent had given statements and two families had taken part in CRP hearings, but had not known this was part of CAVR. These data are consistent with CAVR's outreach, notably that 3–4 per cent of the population engaged with the CRP (Burgess 2004), but inconsistent with the eulogies the Commission has received as an instrument of truth and reconciliation for the nation (e.g. Babo-Soares 2004, Huang and Gunn 2004, Ximenes 2004). These data strongly suggest that the principal mechanisms of the liberal peace perceived as addressing violations of the past are unknown to most victims. Whilst half of those met were insufficiently informed to have an opinion of CAVR, a quarter believed that CAVR had produced no results and 7 per cent believed (falsely) that CAVR had led to their receiving a medal or pension. The product of the Commission is a report that remains largely inaccessible to the ordinary people of Timor-Leste both physically since copies have not reached villages and also due to widespread illiteracy. Even the title of the final report *'Chega!'* is in a language, Portuguese, spoken by only around 2 per cent of the population (Hattori et al. 2005). As the centrepiece of the transitional justice process, CAVR promised truth and reconciliation. The evidence of this study is that it was largely irrelevant to victims of serious crimes. The trope of truth as reconciliation had no resonance with victims interviewed: it was seen that families did not have problems with those in their community linked to violations and the data suggest that reconciliation within communities is largely accomplished. Given the fact that the CRP did not address the issue of the missing or the dead, and that it accessed a very small minority of victims, it seems likely that such reconciliation has either been spontaneous or achieved through community level initiatives. This suggests that in a dispersed rural society such as Timor, processes that emerge organically in communities are far more effective than centralized mechanisms in terms of both accessibility and impact.

As a result of the valorization process, 45 per cent of families met had received a medal, and 13 per cent a pension through the Veterans' Commissions, a process that has been a huge success:

> Yes we are happy [with the medals and pension], it means a history of my father's sacrifice to help free the country; although he is not here with us but this is something that honours him. (Children of missing man, Dili, 16 July 2009)

In addition to the medal itself many families talked with pride of award ceremonies where senior members of the leadership had given them the medals, a clear positive impact on perceptions of legitimacy.

Where Liberal Discourse Meets Indigenous Tradition

An ethnography such as this is able to challenge the culturally-based assumptions that drive approaches to legitimacy. Many of those interviewed in this study do not share ideas of political causation with Western social science and as a result challenge the epistemologies with which we approach how impacts of the conflict can be addressed and thus how legitimacy is perceived. It is a fundamental assumption of social science that there are objective causes of social phenomena: peacebuilding and human rights are constructed on the understanding that changes in law, society and behaviour impact on people in certain ways. An alternative understanding of political causality is that which emerges from a religious or spiritual outlook in which consequences flow, as in the case for Timorese or indigenous Nepalis, from the actions of spirits. Many families interviewed in this study prioritize an addressing of spiritual needs above all others. The wife of a missing man from Lautem, Timor reported:

> ...one of my sons was sick. We brought him to the hospital in Baucau, and he remembered that it [finding his father's body] is something important that we should do. Maybe his sickness is the impact of my husband being missing. Therefore, they went to find his body... [...] we were looking for him because my child was sick, if he had not been sick we would not have found [the body]. (Los Palos, Lautem, 14 August 2009)

A Nepali man whose brother is missing confirmed:

> The first reason the body is important is that we need to perform the ritual ceremony and the second one is to be able declare them as martyrs because they fought for their country. [...] There is nothing else that can satisfy the family; it's difficult because according to the Hindu religion we have to do the death ceremony and it's important as we do it every year. If we don't do it then there is a belief that the spirit of the dead will always trouble the family. (Kathmandu 25 August 2008)

Rural people see their lives as not just influenced but determined in many ways by spirits, whose actions can in turn be affected by human behaviour, notably by the correct performance of ritual. For some families the peace of the nation is dependent upon this, with recent violence in Timor-Leste perceived as arising from the many spirits of the conflict dead still not at rest.

> Sometimes conflict appears in the nation and in villages because of the effect of all the people that died in the forest because of the war. Conflict appears because the nation has not yet recognized the people that died in the war for independence. Conflicts will always appear if the government does not recognize them. (Brother of missing man, Los Palos, Lautem, 13 August 2009)

A failure to acknowledge that conceptions of governance in rural communities emerging from conflict will necessarily diverge from imported global understandings will challenge state legitimacy. The addressing of many of these issues lies not in state institutions, but in traditional hierarchies in the community, where an everyday legitimacy can be constructed that resonates with the political and other communities that are far more valued than those of the remote state.

Towards a Post-liberal Legitimacy

These data challenge a number of the assumptions that underpin the rights-driven mechanisms of the liberal peace in addressing impacts of violence and in constructing legitimacy after conflict. In both Timor-Leste and Nepal, victims overwhelmingly prioritized economic issues and the truth about their missing loved ones. The truth they sought, however, was a private truth, not a public one: the 'therapeutic ethic' (Colvin 2003) of truth as healing (for both individuals and nations) that has driven the Truth Commission as a prescription for addressing legacies of conflict is seen to have been largely irrelevant to victims in its Timorese incarnation. Rather, CAVR confirmed narratives of the Timorese as victims of the Indonesians that resonated with the nation-building needs of the leadership and thus served as regime legitimation for the new Timor-Leste state. This process was almost entirely an elite one, however, with little meaning for ordinary people and victims of the conflict. Yet a need for healing does emerge clearly in these data. The rites required to address spiritual needs are social events that serve as highly visible collective rituals that address community needs for healing. The effectiveness of such ritual derives from its performative nature, echoing the mechanism of truth commissions but using the language of spirit not catharsis and operating in a local social space rather than that of a state institution.

The machinery of liberal peacebuilding in Timor-Leste has been largely invisible to victims of the conflict and effective only where it has delivered something concrete, either in terms of economic support or acknowledgement of the sacrifice of loved ones. Efforts to engage with custom, in terms of traditional dispute resolution incorporated into the work of the CAVR, are largely unknown, representing an instrumentalization that has been romanticized by outside observers but that failed to impact on the vast majority of Timorese. A large number of positive appraisals of the role of the indigenous in the CRP have been written, mainly by those involved in its implementation, through the methodology of studying the very small minority who did engage with it. Such reports were part of the evaluation of the entire peacebuilding process in Timor-Leste that, immediately prior to the violence of 2006, was perceived as having been so successful. The proposed Truth and Reconciliation Commission in Nepal (Government of Nepal 2008) is similarly poised to address elite agendas in the capital, but likely to remain largely invisible in the rural areas where most violations occurred and most Nepalis live. The failure of such mechanisms to have relevance for ordinary people arises precisely from the fact that they emerge not from the local, but from global prescription, legislated from above with little consultation with the population. For process and institutions to aid legitimacy they must be rooted in the everyday social realities with which people live, emphasizing the custom and tradition that have long bound communities together. Such an approach will necessarily permit local particularities, such as the phenomenon of the missing and issues of spirits, to be addressed that are invisible to mimetic global practice.

A strategy to create a locally driven peace can emerge from an analysis of the relationship of the local to the mechanisms and instruments of peacebuilding, by considering the 'modes of inclusion' (Lawoti 2009) of affected populations, including victims of the conflict, in peacebuilding processes. Those examined here (notably CAVR and the judicial process) constitute modes that can best be defined as either instrumentalization or co-option of victims. Intended to add a facade of legitimacy (for example through the fetishization of victim testimony in the truth-telling process of CAVR), they actually serve to ensure the exclusion of affected populations from having agency in such processes. For performance legitimacy to be served by such processes they must at the least be consultative in that they represent a response arising from an effort to understand the views of populations, but at best are participatory and transformative.

Legitimacy as a Function of the Local and Particular

Normative concepts of legitimacy can be traced to Weber's three types of 'legitimate authority': rational–legal, traditional and charismatic (Weber 1978, p. 215). The rational–legal derives mainly from Western concepts of law and is seen to be largely irrelevant in communities that predominantly use their own traditional structures of dispute resolution and find the state judiciary remote and inaccessible. The traditional refers to those customs and structures to which people are accustomed: in Nepal and Timor-Leste local governance, rather than central structures which are at best irrelevant and at worst (as in Timor in Indonesian times) a source of violence and oppression. Charisma refers to perceptions of a leadership but has also been presumed to encompass the provision of goods and services related to state effectiveness (Barakat and Zyck 2009) and thus to include understandings of performance legitimacy. The Weberian framework, however, and the work of those who have attempted to build upon it (Rogowski 1974, Barker 1990, Beetham 1991), have little resonance with the data of this study.

At the level of what Richmond (2009b) calls the 'local-local' in Timor-Leste, efforts of the liberal peace to address the impacts of violence are invisible: they have had no positive impact on victims' perception of their rulers. In Nepal, planned peacebuilding measures appear likely to have similarly little impact outside the capital. For such processes to have an impact on victims there is a need to ensure that they are steered by an understanding of the priorities of local conflict-affected populations and to empower local and indigenous mechanisms that emerge from the local. This represents a *distributed* peace, where the locus of peacebuilding is not in the global offices of international organizations, but in the communities where those most affected by conflict live: a peace that can look different in different parts of the state, subject to both local culture and needs, and the particular impacts of conflict. Ensuring legitimacy for such populations demands a closing of the gap between where the liberal peace is instantiated and communities emerging from conflict.

Whilst it is the Truth Commission of CAVR that has been most praised by observers of Timor-Leste's transition, from the perspective of victims of the conflict the largely ignored valorization process is perceived as by far the most valuable, because it addressed concrete needs. Legitimacy has been described as 'a relatively simple process of meeting people where they are and meeting their needs and expectations' (Barakat *et al.* 2010). 'Meeting people where they are' means both in their communities rather than in remote institutions and in the sense of addressing what they perceive as their priorities. Empirically, legitimacy in the highly collective societies examined here emerges as a shared understanding of the state and political leadership constructed within communities through their perceived interaction with the state. The valorization process succeeded because it addressed victims' needs, namely those for economic support and for recognition in ways that impacted locally, on a significant scale and that were highly visible to the community. The process used currencies that were both understood and valued by the community, namely money and acknowledgement by a charismatic leadership. Reparation was perceived as more important than truth or prosecutions and was most readily delivered to victims through economic support and symbolic recognition, which in addition to sustaining livelihood, served as state acknowledgment of victimhood. Return of the bodies of missing loved ones would be the most reparative and legitimating act of the state, but has yet to happen on any scale in either context.

Conclusion

In contrast to the usual approach of examining what states do in attempts to understand legitimacy, this study has asked those most affected by conflict what they seek to restore a view of the state. The perspectives of victims of conflict have been used to inform conceptions of state legitimacy that are constructed not from global benchmarks but from the everyday priorities of the conflict-affected and reflecting the intrinsically social construction of legitimacy. Empirical studies in two post-conflict states, Nepal and Timor-Leste, confirm that a state's ability to deliver certain services to families and communities drives local concerns. This echoes concepts of *performance legitimacy* that construct perceptions of authority in terms of the perceived effectiveness of the state in addressing needs. For victims in the two states studied those needs considered most important are basic needs, such as can best be satisfied through effective livelihood, and an addressing of the impacts of conflict which, for the families studied here, are dominated by the need for an end to ambiguity about the fate of missing relatives. Victims we met emphasized above all welfare and this, rather than the creation for their own sake of state institutions that will remain remote from them, drives concepts of state legitimacy: performance legitimacy rather than regime legitimacy was prioritized.

The everyday is a space where it can be expected that global norms have to compete with visions of the world rooted in both traditional and highly particular understandings. In the contexts studied here local and indigenous perspectives are seen to exist largely independently of global discourses such as rights. Meanings are constructed collectively in ways that are often unique to the cultures that exist within Timor-Leste and Nepal, and define how both war and peace are perceived and how community is understood: culture has a constitutive role in the initiation and cessation of conflict (Avruch and Black 1987). Similarly, the necessarily collective concept of legitimacy is constructed on local terms, with little reference to the global understandings that benchmark liberal peacebuilding, and any peacebuilding approach that ignores such understandings risks irrelevance to the everyday lives of ordinary people. Whilst basic needs have a degree of universality, many of the everyday impacts on victims emerge directly from local and highly particular social or spiritual understandings. That culture is important, indeed perhaps 'the most important issue of all' (Ramsbotham *et al.* 2005, p. 302) in conflict resolution, is seen in the range of needs that victims articulate in this study and serves to emphasize the centrality of the local and particular to post-conflict legitimacy.

Notes on Contributor

Simon Robins is a humanitarian practitioner and researcher with an interest in transitional justice, humanitarian protection and human rights. He has worked for the International Committee of the Red Cross in conflict and post-conflict contexts, and recently completed a PhD at the Post-war Reconstruction and Development Unit at the University of York on the issue of persons missing in conflict, which remains a focus of his work.

Notes

1 The move to relabel victims as 'survivors', rarely done on the terms of victims, is another example of approaches that reinforce 'victim' as a negative appellation; in this study the identity of victim was perceived as a basis on which claims could be made of the state—the challenge for victims is to deny the dichotomy between victim and agent and attempt to forge a positive and enabling identity.
2 Annual per capita GDP, 2008: Timor-Leste $469; Nepal $444 (World Bank 2010).
3 'Missing persons or persons unaccounted for are those whose families are without news of them and/or are reported missing, on the basis of reliable information, owing to armed conflict (international or non-international) or internal violence' (ICRC 2003).

References

Arbour, L., 2007. Economic and social justice for societies in transition. *NYU journal of international law and politics*, 40, 1–27.
Avruch, K. and Black, P.W., 1987. A generic theory of conflict resolution. *Negotiation journal*, 3 (1), 87–96.

Babo-Soares, D., 2004. Nahe biti: the philosophy and process of grassroots reconciliation (and justice) in East Timor. *The Asia Pacific journal of anthropology*, 5 (1), 15–33.

Barakat, S. and Zyck, S.A., 2009. State building and post-conflict demilitarization: military downsizing in Bosnia and Herzegovina. *Contemporary security policy*, 30 (3), 548–572.

Barakat, S.,Evans, M. and Zyck, S.A., 2010. Karzai's curse: legitimacy as stability in post-conflict environments. Paper presented at the 2010 ISA Conference, New Orleans, LA, 19 February.

Barker, R., 1990. *Political legitimacy and the state*. Oxford: Clarendon Press.

Battachan, K.B., 1998. Making no heads or tails of the ethnic 'conundrum' by scholars with European head and Nepalese tail. *Nepalese studies*, 25 (1), 111–130.

Battachan, K.B., 2006. *Report: indigenous nationalities and minorities of Nepal*. Kathmandu: Tribhuvan University.

Beetham, D., 1991. *The legitimation of power*. Atlantic Highlands, NJ: Humanities Press International.

Boege, V. *et al.*, 2009. Building peace and political community in hybrid political orders. *International peacekeeping*, 16 (5), 599–615.

Brinkerhoff, D.W., 2005. Rebuilding governance in failed states and post-conflict societies; core concepts and cross-cutting themes. *Public administration and development*, 25, 3–14.

Brinkerhoff, D.W., 2007. Introduction—governance challenges in fragile states: re-establishing security, rebuilding effectiveness, and reconstituting legitimacy. *In*: D.W. Brinkerhoff, ed. *Governance in post-conflict societies: rebuilding fragile states*. Oxford: Routledge.

Burgess, P., 2004. Justice and reconciliation in East Timor: the relationship between the Commission for Reception. Truth and reconciliation and the courts. *Criminal law forum*, 15, 135–158.

Call, C. and Cousens, E., 2008. Ending wars and building peace: international responses to war-torn societies. *International studies perspectives*, 9, 1–21.

CAVR (Comissão de Acolhimento, Verdade e Reconciliação de Timor Leste), 2005. *Chega! Final report of the Commission for Reception, Truth and Reconciliation in East Timor*. Dili: CAVR.

Clapham, C., 2003. The global–local politics of state decay. *In*: R. Rotberg, ed. *When states fail: causes and consequences*. Princeton, NJ: Princeton University Press.

Colvin, C.J., 2003. 'Brothers and sisters, do not be afraid of me': trauma, history and the therapeutic imagination in the new South Africa. *In*: K. Hodgkin and S. Radstone, eds. *Contested pasts: the politics of memory*. Oxford: Routledge.

De Alcantara, C.H., 1998. Uses and abuses of the concept of governance. *International social science journal*, 155, 105–113.

François, M. and Sud, I., 2006. Promoting stability and development in fragile and failed states. *Development policy review*, 24 (2), 141–160.

Geertz, C., 1977. *The interpretation of cultures*. New York: Basic Books.

Government of Nepal, 2008. *Draft bill for the establishment of a truth and reconciliation commission*. Kathmandu: Ministry of Peace and Reconstruction.

Government of Timor-Leste, 2010. 2010 census results. Available from: http://timor-leste.gov.tl/?p=4144&n=1&lang=en [Accessed 13 April 2011].

Hachhethu, K., 2003. The question of inclusion and exclusion in Nepal: interface between state and ethnicity. Paper presented to the Conference on 'The Agenda of Transformation: Inclusion in Nepali Democracy' organized by Social Science Baha on 24–26 April, Kathmandu.

Hattori, R. *et al.*, 2005. The ethnolinguistic situation in East Timor. East-West Center working papers, no. 20. Honolulu: East-West Center.

Hayner, P., 2011. *Unspeakable truths: transitional justice and the challenge of truth commissions*. 2nd edn. New York: Routledge.

Höfer, A., 1979. *The caste hierarchy and the state in Nepal. A study of the Muluki Ain of 1854.* Innsbruck: Universitätsverlag Wagner.

Hohe, T. and Nixon, R., 2003. *Reconciling justice: 'traditional' law and state judiciary in East Timor.* Washington, DC: US Institute of Peace.

Huang, R. and Gunn, C., 2004. Reconciliation as state-building in East Timor. *Lusotopie*, 19–38.

Humphrey, M., 2002. *The politics of atrocity and reconciliation: from terror to trauma.* London: Routledge.

INSEC, 2007. *Human rights yearbook 2007.* Kathmandu: INSEC. Summary available from: http://www.inseconline.org/book/Executive%20Summary.pdf [Accessed 13 March 2011].

International Centre for Transitional Justice (ICTJ), 2006. *The serious crimes process in Timor-Leste: in retrospect.* Dili: ICTJ.

International Committee of the Red Cross (ICRC), 2003. *The missing and their families: conclusions arising from events held prior to the International Conference of Governmental and Non-Governmental Experts.* Geneva: ICRC.

International Committee of the Red Cross (ICRC), 2008. *Missing persons in Nepal: the right to know.* Kathmandu: ICRC.

Kent, L., 2005. Community views of justice and reconciliation in Timor-Leste. *Development bulletin*, 68, 62–65.

Kritz, N., 1996. Coming to terms with atrocities: a review of accountability mechanisms for mass violations of human rights. *Law and contemporary problems*, 59, 127–152.

La'o Hamutuk, 2003. Reviewing the East Timor Commission for Reception, Truth and Reconciliation (CAVR). *The La'o Hamutuk Bulletin*, 4 (5). Available from: http://www.laohamutuk.org/Bulletin/2003/Nov/lhv4n5en.pdf [Accessed 5 April 2011].

Lawoti, M., 2009. Dissecting inclusion. *Kathmandu Post*, 3 April.

Madlingozi, T., 2010. On Transitional justice entrepreneurs and the production of victims. *Journal of human rights practice*, 2 (2), 208–228.

Milliken, J. and Krause, K., 2002. State failure, state collapse, and state reconstruction: concepts, lessons and strategies. *Development and change*, 33 (2), 753–774.

Ogura, K., 2008. *Seeking state power—the Communist Party of Nepal (Maoist)* (Berghof Transitions Series No. 3). Berlin: Berghof Research Center for Constructive Conflict Management.

Paris, R., 2004. *At war's end: building peace after civil conflict.* Cambridge: Cambridge University Press.

Ramsbotham, O., Woodhouse, T. and Miall, H., 2005. *Contemporary conflict resolution: the prevention, management and transformation of deadly conflict.* Cambridge: Polity Press.

Richmond, O.P., 2009a. Liberal peace transitions: a rethink is urgent. *Open democracy*, 19 November. Available from: http://www.opendemocracy.net/oliver-p-richmond/liberal-peace-transitions-rethink-is-urgent [Accessed 5 April 2011].

Richmond, O.P., 2009b. Becoming liberal, unbecoming liberalism: liberal–local hybridity via the everyday as a response to the paradoxes of liberal peacebuilding. *Journal of intervention and statebuilding*, 3 (3), 324–344.

Richmond, O.P., 2010. Resistance and the post-liberal peace. *Millennium: journal of international studies*, 38 (3), 665–692.

Richmond, O.P. and Franks, J., 2008. Liberal peacebuilding in Timor Leste: the emperor's new clothes? *International peacekeeping*, 15 (2), 185–200.

Roberts, D., 2011. *Liberal peacebuilding and global governance.* London: Routledge.

Robins, S., 2009. *An assessment of the needs of families of the missing in Nepal.* York: PRDU.

Robins, S., 2010a. Transitional justice as an elite discourse: human rights between the local and the global in post-conflict Nepal. Paper presented at the International Studies Association, New Orleans, February.

Robins, S., 2010b. *An assessment of the needs of families of the missing in Timor-Leste*. York: PRDU.

Robins, S., 2011. Towards victim-centred transitional justice: understanding the needs of families of the disappeared in postconflict Nepal. *International journal of transitional justice*, 5 (1), 75–98.

Rogowski, R., 1974. *Rational legitimacy: a theory of political support*. Princeton, NJ: Princeton University Press.

Rombouts, H., 2002. Importance and difficulties of victim-based research in post-conflict societies. *European journal of crime, criminal law and criminal justice*, 10 (2–3), 216–232.

Simmons, A.J., 2001. *Justification and legitimacy: essays on rights and obligations*. Cambridge: Cambridge University Press.

Staveteig, S., 2007. *How many persons in East Timor went 'missing' during the Indonesian occupation? Results from indirect estimates*. Laxenburg, Austria: International Institute for Applied Systems Analysis.

Stedman, S.J., 1997. Spoiler problems in peace processes. *International security*, 22 (2), 5–53.

Teitel, R.G., 2000. *Transitional justice*. Oxford: Oxford University Press.

Tiwari, B.N., 2007. An assessment of the causes of conflict in Nepal. Paper presented at the Second Annual Himalayan Policy Research Conference Nepal Study Centre, Madison, 11 October.

UN, 2006. Report of the United Nations Independent Special Commission of Inquiry for Timor-Leste. Geneva: UN.

Uprety, L.P., Rai, I. and Sedhain, H.P., 2005. *People-centred advocacy for land tenancy rights in Nepal: a case study of the Community Self-Reliance Centre's grassroots campaign* (Working paper 6). Kathmandu: ActionAid.

Weber, M., 1978. *Economy and society: an outline of interpretive sociology*. Berkeley: University of California Press.

Wilson, R.A., 2001. *The politics of truth and reconciliation in South Africa*. Cambridge: Cambridge University Press.

World Bank, 2008. *Defining heroes: key lessons from the creation of veterans policy in Timor-Leste*. Washington: World Bank.

World Bank, 2010. World Bank databank. Washington: World Bank. Available from: http://databank.worldbank.org/ddp/home.do [Accessed 13 April 2011].

Ximenes, F.B., 2004. *The unique contribution of the community-based reconciliation process in East Timor*. New York: International Center for Transitional Justice and the Institute for Justice and Reconciliation.

Surveying South Sudan: The Liberal, the Local and the Legitimate

David Roberts

The notion of legitimacy in international peacebuilding is an assumed one; there is an expectation that the formal, Weberian state institutions advanced therein will automatically be condoned by those in whose name they are delivered. But such bodies have, since at least colonial times, been suspect in many postconflict spaces and have routinely been ignored, resisted and bypassed when their local propriety does not reflect social preferences, and the empirical evidence does not suggest this pattern has stopped. The persistence of this null legitimacy derives from the exclusionary nature of liberal interventionism, which neither seeks local knowledge from which to design institutions nor considers their requirements important in relation to popular legitimacy. This article uses survey data drawn from Southern Sudan to discuss how legitimacy is seen from within and what it might look like.

Introduction

Both its critics and its advocates argue that liberal peacebuilding interventions are in crisis (Richmond 2009b, Paris 2010). Liberal interventions in their various incarnations—imperialism, postcolonial 'modernization', post-Cold War conditionality, the security–development nexus, postconflict peacebuilding—have rarely achieved the results anticipated and have meandered ideologically and politically over the course of the last half century. Some Western policies have attempted to manipulate postcolonialism into an authoritarian version of the imperial metropolis, some have emphasized a minimal political conditionality and others have most recently favoured a more fundamentalist market approach. Sue Unsworth and Mick Moore (2010, p. 6) remind us that external authority has emphasized

> in quick succession, ... state-led development, then liberalisation, privatisation and the retrenchment of government from core functions, followed by 'bringing the state back in', democratization, decentralization, the establishment of

autonomous agencies, the creation of public–private partnerships, and civil society participation in the delivery of core services.

Few, if any, have presented 'development' or 'peace' other than from an authoritarian liberal perspective: social evolution has been on very foreign terms, even where local actors and elites have supported them (Richmond 2009, Chandler 2010). Contemporary postconflict peacebuilding, top-down in nature and emphasizing the minimalist state framing market determinism, is the latest in a line of social engineering fads aimed at replicating 'Westernity'. Thus, modern peacebuilding, as with its 'development' precedent, falls into what Isaiah Berlin called 'authoritarian' peace, because in elevating centralized, metropolitan political institutions, no account is made of what subnational heterogeneous groups of local people might want their governments to prioritize. They get what they are given. Postconflict peacebuilding advances external preferences whilst retarding internal influence through ideological hegemony and economic determinism. Liberal peacebuilding denies choice and forestalls the kind of peace a citizenry might choose for themselves, leaving peace lacking sufficient internal, local dimension beyond momentary participation in technical processes like elections and Truth Commissions. Given this mismatch between external and internal preferences, it is unsurprising that the empirical record shows a substantial failure on the part of liberal peacebuilding to build liberal or sustainable peace. It also reveals, however, alternatives that lie at the interface of orthodox and critical literatures.

The Evidence

The persistence of orthodox peacebuilding might imply to some that it brings peace and liberalizes societies. But the record would not uphold such a conclusion. Soberingly, Keith Krause and Oliver Jutersonke (2005, p. 448) note that 'about half of all peace support operations (including both peacekeeping and more expansive peacebuilding operations) fail after around five years', with recurring violence acting as the key indicator of policy bankruptcy. They argue that postconflict peacebuilding 'is littered with states (Afghanistan, Somalia, Liberia, Angola, Haiti and even Cambodia) in which domestic governance is weak, armed violence remains high, and respect for human rights and the rule of law is questionable' (Krause and Jutersonke 2005, p. 449). Other scholars sustain such general criticisms, pointing to the failure of liberal peacebuilding to build durable peace and liberal institutions and political behaviour in (for example) Afghanistan (Howella and Linda 2009, Ledwidge 2011); Angola (Wilson 2004, McMillan 2005); the Congo (Afoaku 2005, Autesserre 2010); Somalia (Le Sage 2002); Liberia (Boas 2001); Sierra Leone (Boas 2001, Fanthorpe 2005); Uganda (Cammack 2007); Eritrea and Ethiopia (Weinstein 2005); El Salvador (Snyder 2000); and Bosnia and Herzegovina (Chandler 1999; Sorensen 2002).

Fleshing out the critique further, critics complain the outcome is less liberal democracy and more 'feckless pluralism' (Carothers 2002), an outcome famously characterized by Fareed Zakaria (1997) as 'illiberal democracy'. Elaborating on such critiques, Marina Ottaway (2002) charges that most elites after 'democratization' and 'liberalization' are semi-authoritarian rather than democratic or liberal. David Chandler (1999) and Jens Sorensen (2002) illustrate Ottaway's point with regard to the Balkans, and Pierre Lizee (2000) and Stephen Heder (1995) affirm the paucity of liberalism in Cambodia. According to such critics, postconflict polities often barely sustain Dahl's (1971) notion of 'minimal democracy'. More recently, in Southern Sudan, a report from the London School of Economics (LSE) maintains that, in addition to internal causes of recurrent post-settlement violence, liberal, Weberian statebuilding priorities are actually undermining peace. This is because the

> state-building approach ... has prioritized building government capacity to deliver services in the future over more instant service delivery. As a result, communities and individuals committing violence feel they have little to lose through violent behaviour. In common with most Liberal peacebuilding, external peacebuilding in Southern Sudan is detached from the internal reality that might well guide more relevant peace locally. (Schomerus and Allen 2010, p. 10)

The Theories

In the identification of 'problems' and in the search for 'solutions', opinion has polarized. Advocates of the liberal orthodoxy concede that the Liberal Project, as Tom Young (1994) called it, is not securing the south for local or northern rationales as it was expected to. Their solution involves refining the prevailing approach using the same methodologies based on existing ontological assumptions (Chesterman 2004); such scholarship proposes more technical solutions for what are primarily political matters. Its imaginary can be summarized as more of the same, ordered differently and more firmly applied. The emphasis in this view remains on security sector reform, Weberian institutions and market economics (Call 2008). Critical literature, however, challenges the ontological and epistemological foundations of the 'top-down' and external emphasis, proposing instead 'emancipation' and the idea of 'the everyday'. Such thinking advances the need for greater emancipation from structural violence, some degree of indigenous autonomy in determining peacebuilding priorities, and the idea of the 'everyday' as a focal point for 'post-liberal' or fourth generation peacebuilding.

For Oliver Richmond (2008, p. 109), for example, fourth generation peacebuilding reflects 'the interests, identities, and needs of all actors, state and non-state', through 'the creation of a discursive framework of mutual accommodation and social justice which recognizes difference'. Elaborating further, he suggests this departure from orthodoxy focuses

> on the question of how one can move beyond the installation of a hegemonic peace, and move towards an everyday notion of peace sensitized to the local as well as the state, regional and global... resting upon a just social order and solidarity, transcending that offered by the liberal peace. (Richmond 2008, p. 109)

The 'everyday' refers here to the informal social routines of daily existence that people use to get what they need when faced with extreme contingencies. These imaginings 'offer a vision of an emancipatory, everyday and empathetic form of peace in the context of a post-conventional, post-Westphalian IR' (Richmond 2008, p. 131). They are concerned with the idea of a peace which is not necessarily contingent on sovereign territoriality, does not necessarily privilege the traditional organs and priorities of modern statebuilding, and involves a wider range of ordinary people in the shaping of a more positive and far-reaching peace that reflects their needs and priorities, in whatever peaceful form this takes. Fourth generation perspectives are context-specific, driven by people's needs and prioritize the concept of the everyday, theorizing a 'post-liberal' peace that shifts the prevailing emphasis away from external hegemony to the recognition of the importance, centrality and utility of the 'local' in peace-building—without inappropriately romanticizing indigeneity or forgetting its complexity and polarity (Liden *et al.* 2009, Mac Ginty 2010).

Although both schools have very different ontological drivers with equally divergent policy proposals, they both acknowledge the importance of legitimacy. Predictably, however, their perspectives on this matter are very different. The orthodoxy prioritizes the internalization and habituation of new political norms conforming to the external world of global governance institutions, audited benchmarks and political values like accountability, transparency, the separation of powers and elected executives. Legitimacy is from this perspective mainly through a very liberal lens (Gilley 2009). It is assumed that it is possible for the kind of international institutions involved in peacebuilding to be effective and achieve their objectives without needing or seeking local legitimacy (Symons 2010). The prevailing emphasis, in both the literature and the field, is on external legitimacy, notwithstanding the rhetoric of 'participation' afforded by processes like elections and truth commissions. The 'citizens' which the Weberian state seeks to govern are not consulted as to what that state should be doing, leaving a gap between legitimacy and the local, the international system and the legitimate state, and the literature and sustainable peace. The critical perspective argues that for interventions to deliver peace, the institutions prioritized in peacebuilding must have relevance and legitimacy at the local level. In this view, persistent ignoring of the importance of internal legitimacy is maintained at the peril of peacebuilding. Local legitimacy is not being sought, but it is clearly needed, critical scholars argue, for peace, liberal or otherwise, to evolve. Jean Leca (1990, p.60) summarized the dissonance well when he argued that 'the legitimacy of a democratic government does not depend only on the practice of democracy but above all on what the people get from the rulers'. The liberal emphasis on the technical elements to democratization persists at the expense of the political economy of popular demand.

This article is concerned, then, 'to comprehend ... what makes sense to people at the local level without prior ideological or theoretical agenda' (Chabal 2009, p. 173). The research question must then be: what kind of peacebuilding, internal and external, with which emphases and which institutions and services, might be considered legitimate, and thence more sustainable, to heterogeneous postconflict populations? Embedded in this question is a different epistemology that recognizes the limits to the knowledge of international peacebuilders, which can best be expanded by referring to those in whose name liberal peacebuilding is undertaken. It should be made quite clear at this point that this is not an exercise to determine what is legitimate in terms of postconflict development. This is an exercise in determining what validates the peacebuilding interventions themselves in the eyes of local people. The purpose of this research is to identify the terms and conditions upon which postconflict societies consent to be governed. It is not to be confused with establishing development agendas and priorities, although these may overlap. It concerns postconflict stabilization and the means by which reciprocating respect between state and society can create a stable political context within which peaceful development may occur.

Legitimacy, the Local and the Global

What do we mean when we talk of legitimacy? These debates have been held in innumerable locations in broad terms, occupying a key tranche of philosophical and political literatures spanning centuries; as postcolonialism evolves, and those debates have been reconsidered and reinterpreted through a variety of lenses in the development literature. But the question of the nature and meaning of political legitimacy is more of a stranger in the field of postconflict peacebuilding, since it has been ordered by a liberal hegemony convinced of the universal virtue of the 'privileging of universal over local knowledge [and] the privileging of international over domestic sources of legitimacy' (Chabal 2009, p. 4).

A different view emerges, however, which argues that, whilst there is nothing necessarily wrong with liberal values per se, the favoured and prioritized liberal institutions that are advanced to reproduce those values and associated behaviours may not be appropriate to all postconflict places. This is not the argument that suggests people in such places are in some way not 'ready' for democracy, a patronizing claim well critiqued by David Chandler (2010a). Instead, this work is concerned with what a state would have to do to be accepted by the people over whom it claims jurisdiction and from whom it requires public sanction. In this sense, we reach a watershed. On the one side, legitimacy has been comported in terms of what it can do for international actors without reference to how legitimacy is composed in order to sanction the state to the people (in the classical liberal tradition of the social contract). The other side of the watershed concerns a time to think about what political legitimacy, of elites, institutions and priorities might mean, if anything, to the people in whose name peacebuilding and democratization are imagined.

The Local Context

The abstract theorizing common to academia in general and to the peacebuilding debate in particular often acts to cloud the social reality in postconflict spaces. In most, jobs, water, roads and electricity (to name but a few) are in short supply but of great importance to local people. Mark Duffield (2008) has compellingly referred to the difference between the two worlds—of the global from whence directives come and the local within which they are received—as 'insured' and 'uninsured'. Thus, what might appear to be relevant or, most likely, a priority from the viewpoint of Paris, Washington or Sydney may not seem so in Luanda, Kathmandu or Bujumbura, cities teeming with very poor people chasing employment and coming out of war. Furthermore, Luanda, Kathmandu and Bujumbura are not representative of the wider populations of those countries; conditions in capital cities are normally substantially different from those of the surrounding environs. As government spokesman Khieu Kanharith (1998, p. 6) put it in the wake of the largest UN peacebuilding intervention of the last century, 'Phnom Penh is not Cambodia'. International and national metropolitan priorities, preferences and interests will not be likely to mirror those of the wider heterogeneous societies that normally stabilize or destabilize political authority. This is not to claim that international peacebuilders are unaware of local conditions, but those conditions rarely govern international peacebuilders' agendas.

Thus, core functions in liberal states, like refuse collection, mains power or street lighting, whose absence or withdrawal would probably provoke a riot in Europe, are rarely even minimally present in postconflict spaces, even in metropolitan centres. Indeed, years after UN intervention and peacebuilding, there was little or no reliable mains electricity or waste collection in either Cambodia or Sierra Leone, both of which were initially considered successes (Roberts 2011). Furthermore, those who make and implement peacebuilding policy have rarely experienced the consequences of such conditions over the long term; obvious pressures and contingencies on ordinary people, like basic survival, are routinely overlooked or ignored in peacebuilding practices (Roberts 2001, Peake and Scheye 2005). People whose basic interests, needs, preferences and priorities are ignored by the governments they elect in UN polling are unlikely to see such polities as credible, engendering a legitimacy vacuum. Even where security sector reform (SSR) has been advanced in line with basic requirements from both internal and external viewpoints, too much of the time it is more the state that has been secured, and less the society. SSR, like much of liberal interventionism, is primarily a technical process that avoids engagement with the wholly more complex local and global political economies of disarmament, reintegration and police reform, resulting in, among other things, new uniforms and training for the constabulary but no consideration of how such agents of the state will feed their families when the state is told to contract for efficiency. Eighteen years after the UN left Cambodia, police officers on Achar Mean Boulevard in clean, new uniforms on expensive police motorcycles carrying recently distributed repression equipment and telecommunications equipment from European suppliers still laugh when they are asked why they have not stopped extorting cash from poor local people. They cannot all be bad people; their uniforms and retraining have been provided at considerable cost but half-decent salaries too often have not, and their political loyalty to various powerful individuals (as opposed to the state) has not been touched. Similar stories are to be heard in Sierra Leone, Afghanistan, Iraq and Timor-Leste, to mention but a few (Pugh 2002, Peake and Scheye 2005, Jalali 2006, Egnell and Halden 2009); all show a failure of the fundamental liberal mandate to move the personal to the professional, the informal to the formal. This is unsurprising; liberal peacebuilding does not engage well with local complexity.

Rethinking Legitimacy in Postconflict Societies

Whilst such exclusion and neglect has occupied much orthodox peacebuilding scholarship, it is not to say nobody has been thinking hard in terms of the local. Some writers, like Moniker Francois and Inder Sud (2006), for example, have described the form of legitimacy associated with what local people might prioritize if their voices were heard as 'performance' legitimacy. It should of course be noted that the test of legitimacy for the 'global' is already based on its performance, but in relation to external prerogatives. However, the term is applied by Francois and Sud to the local in terms of delivery. Concerned with similar matters, Merilee Grindle reminds us a question posed by Jean Leca (1990, pp. 60, 174), who asked: 'how can participative democracy be encouraged if paternalistic authoritarianism and/or 'amoral familism' seems more effective?'. Grindle posits that in order to acquire legitimacy, newly-minted governments and their associated institutions in postconflict spaces must

> ensure the regular provision of basic public goods, such as order, security, and legitimate authority. Governments have to develop public health infrastructure and ensure that all citizens receive basic services in health and education. They have to be able to protect the basic rights of their populations and encourage their political participation. (Grindle 2004, p. 546)

Drawing similar conclusions, even if primarily concerned with the security of the US rather than of postconflict states per se, Stuart Eizenstat, John Edward Porter and Jeremy Weinstein (2005) argue in *Foreign Affairs* that provision of things like health and education are essential to the legitimacy and stability of a weak state. And in a British government-funded ten-year research programme, the Institute of Development Studies (IDS) concluded in 2010 that the weak states characteristic of postconflict spaces needed to emphasize political security and legitimacy within their own environs if stability and peace were to be achieved (Unsworth and Moore 2010). They went on to argue that peacebuilders should not 'try to sell a preconceived reform agenda based on Western models [and should] be open to unorthodox ways in which elements of public authority are in practice being created, often in unexpected ways' (Unsworth and Moore 2010, p. 15). Grindle suggests that we need better data from within to better order and organize government in relation to a viable, durable peace. Grindle (2004, p. 538) remarks that:

> Producing tangible benefits in the short term might be a wise first step for many governments, particularly those suffering from reform fatigue or weak legitimacy. For example, improving garbage collection in poor neighborhoods and providing more security in public markets are high visibility changes that can build citizen trust that government services are getting better.

She adds that:

> Priorities can be better set if there is more understanding about which actions produce more results in terms of efficiency, effectiveness, and responsiveness; which produce the most benefit for the poor; which logically precede others; which are easier to undertake or produce results in the short term; and under what conditions particular reforms are likely to have the most impact. While assessing the administrative and fiscal capacity of countries to carry through on various commitments is important, setting priorities for actions requires a broader frame of reference. (Grindle 2004, p. 537)

Would such an approach contribute to the development of political legitimacy through a balanced social contract? This method clearly diverges from the prevailing convention; but the 'unorthodox ways of public authority' are vague and lack more precise definition. Perhaps the problem of epistemology and ontology remains, since it is outsiders, albeit well-informed and experienced ones, who are making such propositions. The following section looks at empirical data that might lead somewhere else in terms of identifying what might constitute legitimacy, but it also problematizes local interpretation of the very concept itself.

Empirical Data?

A 2002 survey in Africa undertaken by Afrobarometer, a respected survey instrument, concerned with 'countries that have introduced a measure of democratic and market reforms over the last decade', found a very broad preference for democracy over authoritarianism. It also found that:

> When asked about the features of 'a democratic society', almost everyone (89 percent) thinks it important that citizens have access to the basic necessities of life (like food, water and shelter). In practice, people want democracy to deliver these benefits, including education, even more strongly than they insist on regular elections, majority rule, competing political parties, and freedom to criticize the government (all about 75 percent). Thus, Africans are predisposed to judge the performance of democracy primarily in terms of its record at delivering improvements in the socioeconomic sphere. (Afrobarometer 2002, p. 2)

Rightly or wrongly, the people surveyed connoted 'democracy' and the process of democratization, in which different actors determine which aspects of democracy they prefer and when, with quite immediate socio-economic priorities that were, inevitably, related to the nature of politics and ideology. That survey is dated, but it reveals a disconnect between stated social priorities and state activity.

That message persisted in the 2008 Afrobarometer survey of 19 African states in political journeys similar to those faced in orthodox peacebuilding. This survey found that a substantial majority (66 per cent) of African people surveyed considered that their 'government's economic policies have hurt most people and only benefited a few' (Little and Logan 2008, p. 38). When asked if their governments were performing 'fairly/very well' or 'fairly/very poorly' in the area of 'improving the living standards of the poor', about twice the number of respondents agreed with the latter (Little and Logan 2008, p. 21). A general (but not absolute) trend appears as an acceptance of the constitutional principles of democratic governance such as the right to rule and the rule of law; but with a concomitant belief that anointed governments are not effectively providing for the poorest people, who often constitute a substantial majority of the population. It was a majority view (more than 50 per cent) that 'local governance' was viewed as underperforming in areas such as 'allowing citizens… to participate in the council's decisions' or ensuring that 'local government revenues are used for public services and not for private gain' (Little and Logan 2008, p. 24). These can be interpreted as comments on the nature of democracy itself in terms of ownership and participation, and upon corruption in the system. Given how the respondents claimed to feel about this, it is thus unsurprising that over half considered that 'the amount of influence traditional leaders have in governing [their] local community should increase' (Little and Logan 2008, p. 28). This presents a contradiction when it occurs in the peacebuilding context, in the sense that unrepresentative democracy is a self-fulfilling prophecy, since where the state neglects what people see as its responsibility, they abdicate from the social contract in favour of the informal processes democratization is meant to change.

Narrowing the review to research undertaken in postconflict spaces experiencing liberal development as a means of peacebuilding, the data is yet scarcer, but a similar picture emerges of mixed views, poor local performance and reliance on traditional institutions and processes, especially in rural areas. Regarding Sierra Leone, for example, Edward Sawyer (2008) notes a reversion to the informal chiefdoms in rural and urban Sierra Leone responsible in part for the long-running war. Commenting on this tendency, Richard Fanthorpe (2005, p. 45; also see Williams 2004) argues that:

> one size fits all institutional remedies may blind practitioners to the political imperatives that bind the rural poor to non-liberal modes of governance and therefore leave hastily erected 'democratic' institutions vulnerable to political capture by the very forces the project seeks to thwart.

Similar conclusions were drawn from a study in Southern Sudan (Schomerus and Allen 2010, p. 82), Azerbaijan (O'Lear 2007), Angola (Wilson 2004), Nepal (Askvik et al. 2011), Somaliland (Jhazbhay 2009) and Afghanistan (Rennie et al. 2008). Dependence on informal practices and social institutions remains commonplace in such postconflict spaces, as it has done in developing countries not managing the detritus of war, in part because the priorities, corruption and impotence of centralized government necessitate such relations; in part because the metropolis tends to ignore the periphery except where it can exploit its resources or where it decides it must be disciplined; and in part because there is no formal, effective and accessible substitute for informal practices and institutions for millions of very poor people. The Spartan nature of the data suggests that there is good reason to undertake further empirical research in postconflict spaces; the following section notes a few methodological implications for such an approach before introducing the outcome of a 2011 survey in Southern Sudan.

Methodological Considerations

Researchers working in highly maldeveloped societies, impoverished by civil and international war, by corrupt and despotic government or by unfair global trade systems will find much in common in very diverse places. Routinely, infrastructure conditions prevent extensive travel beyond metropolitan centres. In Cambodia, Liberia, Sierra Leone, Nepal and Southern Sudan, for example, there are few sealed roads beyond the capitals and local transport may often be unreliable and usually physically painful over any length of time. When travel is better facilitated by peacebuilding interventions (UN helicopters and rigid inflatable boats, for example), research may be compromised by language barriers and a lack of translators able and willing to spend long periods in unfamiliar places distant from families and relative safety (Devereux and Hoddinott 1993, Schomerus and Allen 2010). Furthermore, even external support does not guarantee that communications remain reliable once in place; bridges collapse in rains, roads may be swept away and locations lost in the process. When transport has been secured in whatever form, through formal external support or informal internal customs, there is normally the security situation to consider, since few cantonments and demobilizations go smoothly, and banditry in military or civilian form exists as a matter of course beyond the reach of state forces, many of which are responsible for armed robbery in the first place.

In addition, if the researcher stays in or returns to the relative stability of the metropolis, he or she often faces the extreme accommodation costs incumbent on the inflation that accompanies UN peacebuilding interventions, ramped up further by massive per diem payments. If illnesses are avoided or fought off, transport arranged and language matters mastered as far as they can be, researchers will often find themselves confronted by unreasonable expectations in gathering their data (political interviewees demanding cash for questions, for example), different attitudes towards communication and meetings, and poorly-mapped geographies and out of date maps, all in a climate that can be quite physically debilitating at various points in the calendar. Such challenges have been well-considered by Devereux and Hoddinott (1993) and Britha Mikkelsen (2005) amongst others.

In broad terms, Merilee Grindle (2004, p. 526) summarized conditions in very poor places (few if any postconflict spaces are wealthy) thus:

> Almost by definition their institutions are weak, vulnerable, and very imperfect; their decision-making spaces are constricted by the presence of international actors with multiple priorities, their public organizations are bereft of resources and are usually badly managed; those who work for government are generally poorly trained and motivated. Frequently, the legitimacy of poor country governments is questionable; their leadership may be venal and their commitments to change undermined by political discord; their civil societies may be disenfranchised, deeply divided, and ill-equipped to participate effectively in politics.

Such conditions are common in postconflict spaces. For many policymakers hailing from secure environments, conditions are, without exaggeration, unimaginable for many. Thus, whilst in many instances and as a prevailing norm the Western mindset turns automatically to the challenges of democratization, for many local people whose everyday lives are predominantly affected by such conditions, other matters may take primacy. The daily endurance tests of collecting and cleansing water from water sources miles from home, and of hard field labour in unstable geographies polluted by unexploded ordnance and crippling levels of child and maternal mortality, are often as remote from the metropolis as they are from the policies that will determine their future lives.

In addition, there are substantial challenges in how, once data has been collated, they are interpreted between cultures, a problem reviewed by Martin Bulmer and Donald Warwick (1993) and by Vandana Desai and Robert Potter (2006); and by the questions of what to research and the extent to which social research in the Global South can be sustained with subjective approaches (Beckford 1983, Fuller 1992). There is, as some of the critical literature noted above suggests, both an ontological and epistemological shift required in recognizing peace as a plural concept, and coexisting pluralities of peace (the liberal, the other) are underpinned by plural epistemologies. The 'knowledge' from which liberal peace scholars extract their theories, methods, policies and practices derives mainly from without, whilst knowledge regarding other forms and priorities of peace derive mainly from within. In short, understanding peace locally requires a different epistemology and supporting research methodology than does understanding peace globally. It was in this context that primary research was conducted in Southern Sudan between April and June 2011.

Southern Sudan

Until 2005, when the Comprehensive Peace Agreement (CPA) was signed, Sudan had been at war for several decades (Schomerus and Allen 2010, Sidahmed 2010). In the wake of the CPA, a popular referendum confirmed that the country should be divided; the outcome, declared in 2011, was the emergence of a 'new' country, to be presided over by the eponymous Government of Southern Sudan (GOSS). Conditions are challenging. The World Bank notes that in Southern Sudan:

> In addition to basic insecurity and food shortages, there are no paved roads outside the major towns. Laying of land mines along key transit routes has left communities isolated and unable to market their goods. Bridges have collapsed and traditional trade links with neighbouring countries disrupted. In a region where per capita income is less than $100, and access to basic social services amongst the lowest in the world, people's expectations for a tangible peace dividend are high. (Klugman and Kallau 2009)

With such matters taken into consideration, a survey was launched in March concerned with identifying what the people of Southern Sudan wanted their government to do for them first. The research was carried out under the aegis of the National Democratic Institute (NDI), an international peacebuilding actor engaged with local needs and voices, across all ten states of Southern Sudan, using up to 67 focus groups involving approximately 700 people who were broadly representative across state, location, tribe, section, religion, gender, age group and education level. The numbers are imprecise because not all the members of all the focus groups would respond to all the questions of the survey. Locations were well-known and had been visited before, and respondents knew in advance of the survey, were familiar with the functioning of the research exercise and had developed trust bonds with those involved in its implementation. They are not strictly statistically representative because of the logistics, costs and challenges involved in postconflict conditions as severe as those common to Southern Sudan. The survey sought to identify common themes and issues that South Sudanese raised repeatedly across the various divisions, and to highlight where there was no common theme. The data was accumulated over a ten week period between March and June 2011. Of a total budget of $75,000 for this survey, $65,000 went on flights, car rental and accommodation for the moderators and enumerators.

Three questions regarding legitimacy and public preferences were added to an existing survey. For the first question, respondents were asked to indicate what they thought was most important for the government to focus on: democracy, development or both simultaneously. The most apparent finding from this question was that democracy was interpreted very subjectively and sometimes not in ways that external peacebuilders would recognize. In the second question, respondents were asked to identify what they wanted their governments to deliver first, second and third from a list of seven preferences. Respondents were also given the option of identifying and proposing additional priorities, reflecting the methods deployed in an earlier survey of Southern Sudan led by the highly-regarded LSE, and concerned with not dissimilar matters (Schomerus and Allen 2010). This produced a fairly clear hierarchy of preferences, shown below. The third question asked respondents how they would judge the success of their government in five years' time. This was conceptually unfamiliar to both enumerators and respondents, who, in common with many other people in postconflict spaces, have rarely considered whether a centralized government should be held accountable to the will of the populace. The data from this question is not deployed in this work because it was clear that it was too ambiguous to be useful.

Some critics have suggested that the second question, asking respondents to rank their preferences from a list provided by the researcher via the enumerator, substitutes one external agenda with another. It is true that, once more, this research inquiry has come from without. However, the logic of the various components has been distilled from development scholarship of the last 50 years undertaken in analogous conditions; from 20 years of fieldwork experience in postconflict spaces; and from various hierarchies of basic needs, most of which are vital to human survival but many of which are often too inaccessible for millions of people in the wake of war. The data from the survey is transparently stored and disseminated. (The raw survey results can be accessed at http://www.popularpeace.org.) Tabulated data and graphs are also accessible from this site in Excel and PowerPoint form with no charge and no copyright restriction. A sample of the data appears here, but the complete original data can be manipulated in various software packages to provide other, more specific results.

Questions and Results:

Q1. Which do you think is more important for the government to focus on first—making sure that South Sudan is a democracy OR making sure that development is happening as fast as possible?

Democracy	37.7
Development	59.1
Democracy and Development Simultaneously	3.2

This data initially appears to imply a substantial preference amongst participants for development to take place before democratization, where both are broadly understood in loose terms. Many reasons were given, but key to this

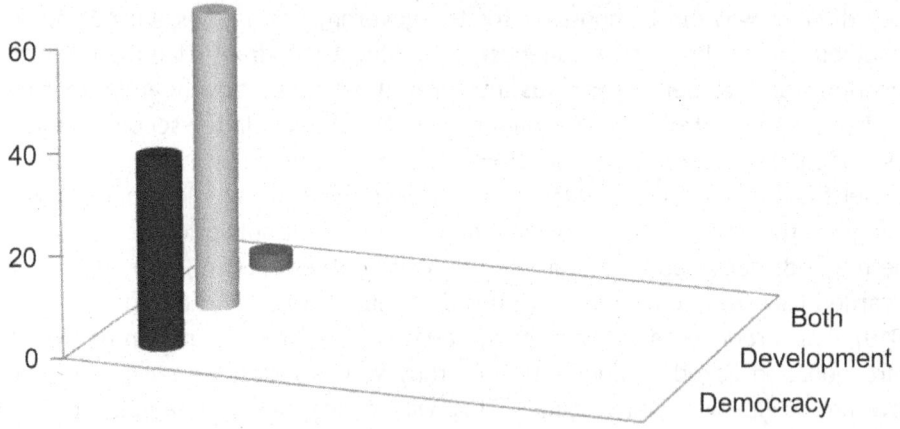

Figure 1. Preferences for democracy and development

rationale was the notion that conditions were so severe that basic needs had to be taken care of before politics in distant urban centres. Those who favoured democratization and political institutionalization before social and economic development tended to be younger, male, urban, with slightly higher education levels. However, several chiefs' groups (made up of older, less-educated males in rural areas) held the same view. A Christian male in Juba educated to primary school level, for example, expressed his rationale clearly, arguing that 'with democracy, the government will hear the will of the people and then [be able to] bring about development'. A Dinka Christian male educated to secondary level claimed that democracy should come first because democratic polities produced faster development. The same individual suggested that conflict and maldevelopment had befallen Libya because it was undemocratic, whilst in Jonglei Akobo a Nuer male declared that democracy 'should come first because it will come with freedom' and would act as a 'foundation' for development. A key concern commonly expressed was that democracy had to come first to deal with 'tribalism' in the government. This was often a concern regarding alleged Dinka domination of the government and civil service, for example.

Those who favoured development before democracy were equally sure of their positions. In Lakes Cueibet Mayath, an older Dinka female declared that 'development should be brought first [because] it is better for the government to make sure that food is available first because without food there is no stability'. A younger Lokloko male in Western Bahr el Ghazal argued that the price of not developing would be paid in the rejection of democracy. One older Muslim Lokloko male claimed that 'if every place gets developed, there would be no rejection of democracy but if there is no development, government would fail'. A Christian female in Western Bahr el Ghazal favoured development 'because we have just come out of war', while another said they had yearned for democracy for so long but it had never come, so development should be prioritized instead.

The main problem with concluding that democracy is more or less important than development is that there was no agreement on what democracy was. Whilst most people had an unequivocal interpretation of development, which is broadly in line with how the United Nations Development Programme and various other international development bodies see it, people's interpretation of democracy varied widely, in accordance with the range of elements of which it is constituted. In addition, their expressions of democracy often overlapped with development. For example, whilst some saw democracy in terms of human rights like freedom of speech, a free media and multi-partyism, others saw it in terms of human rights connected to the right to life, to water or to education. Whilst many identified the right to vote freely, others identified democracy with the right to an education and early years vaccines. In the end, the question was not as helpful as it might have been if a more specific expression of democracy had been advanced. As it transpires, such a nebulous area of discussion enlivened debate and encouraged participation in the survey. Enumerators reported that this paved the way for a lively and vigorous response to the second question, as well as the first.

Q2. I will read you a list. Please tell me which would be the first area you'd want the government to address, the second area and the third area?
Clean water; Electricity; Jobs; Roads; Housing; Healthcare; Education; Any Other Area of Development [NAME THE AREA.]

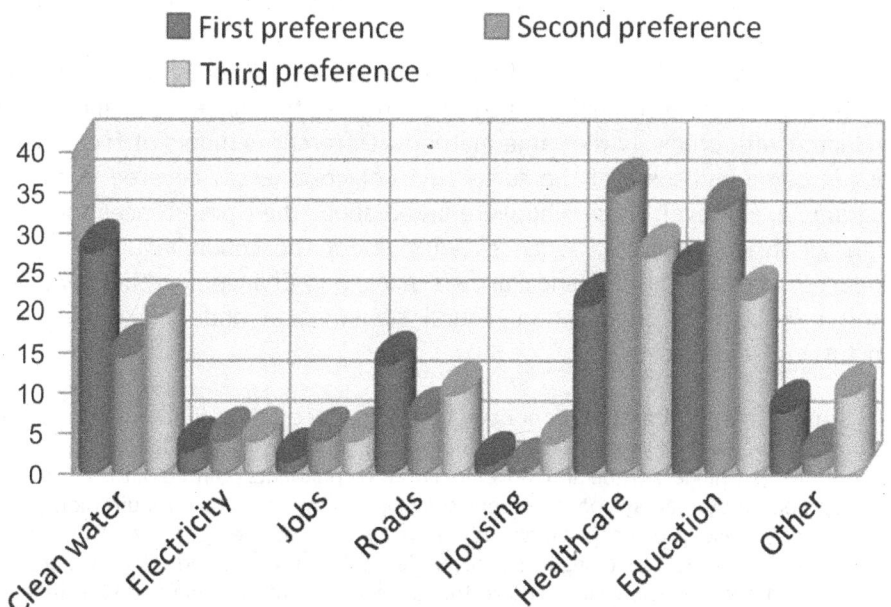

Figure 2. Public priorities for peacebuilders

Government service	First choice	Second choice	Third choice
Water	27.5	14.6	19.5
Electricity	2.9	4.1	4.1
Jobs	1.5	4.1	4.1
Roads	13.6	6.7	9.8
Housing	1.1	.4	3.8
Healthcare	20.9	35.1	27.1
Education	24.9	32.8	21.8
Other	7.7	2.2	9.8

There was significant variation within and between regions and identities, as is to be expected. But the most significant first choice was access to clean water, with education coming second and healthcare third. Water was the third preference of almost one-fifth of the population that responded and healthcare and education the second priority of more than a third of the sample. Thus, whilst there was great diversity across the survey, common themes emerge. First, political democracy was less important than basic development for a majority of those surveyed. Second, in terms of development, the most popular priorities were water, health and education. This is not to suggest peacebuilders should provide water; but they might be engaged with local authorities in mobilizing such important basics. Third, none of these are contemporary postconflict peacebuilding priorities and, indeed, postconflict reconstruction lending conditions are based on a preference for market provision of such priorities. This means that not only are basic necessities not part of the social contract between emergent states and the societies from whom they derive their authority and legitimacy, but also that prime opportunities to build meaningful and durable relations between people and parliaments continue to be missed after the peacebuilders leave.

The findings are corroborated to some degree by another primary research programme in Southern Sudan. It did not address all the same issues and was not conducted with precisely the same methods. Different numbers of focus groups were involved and some of the survey did not cover areas covered in the NDI programme. However, those who were asked about their preferences for peace often identified similar dissonances with liberal peacebuilding. The survey, conducted through the LSE and Partners Achieving Change Together (PACT), a noted development organization, found similar data and drew comparable conclusions. It declared:

> It is clear from almost all interviews that better access to services is seen as a vital ingredient of peace. Lack of development in infrastructure impacts quality of life as it hinders trade and movement, but respondents pointed out that being connected by road symbolized more than simple infrastructure requirement. In parts [of one province], being able to travel along the road was the most remarkable aspect of being at peace, while in Raja County, one religious leader pointed out that the road was also the gateway for information and knowledge both desperately needed by the Southern Sudanese to become informed citizens. (Schomerus and Allen 2010, p. 71)

Legitimacy and Ambiguity

Inevitably, the discourse is not as simple as a basic dichotomy between interpretations of democracy and development, or between the local and the global. What becomes clearer is a different conversation about legitimacy, which resonated with other primary fieldwork in Cambodia, Nepal, Sierra Leone, Somaliland, Viet Nam and other places. The discourses framing legitimacy only in terms of an unambiguous expression of either global or local legitimacy misses the ambiguity with which the concept is viewed from both locations. The literature concerning exogenous, top-down, Weberian, state-centric institutional legitimacy emphasizing the global is as divided as the material concerned with indigenous, bottom-up formal and informal processes emphasizing the local. But in addition, there is the idea that affording legitimacy to the state is itself is a querulous and questionable construct. It misses the notion that for many there is no assumption either way. This has a long and well-documented tradition in the imperial and postcolonial eras, and in some respects this tradition persist today, simultaneously bypassing and undermining the emphasis currently placed on the state in postconflict peacebuilding.

Although many imperial and postcolonial governments were routinely a violent, authoritarian force within a speciously-defined territory, they could not be considered legitimate because the idea of sovereign and metropolitan leadership was devoid of local context and history; lacking in a relational setting, distant and not given status except under duress (Amin 1977, Englebert 2002). These regimes' administrations were usually ignored as long as they did not bother people and the reach of any authority declined quickly with geographical distance from the metropolitan centre (Amin 1977). Equally, however, such regimes might not necessarily be considered illegitimate, because there was only limited expectation in the first place that such a political entity existed to serve local people or generate an enduring social contract (Vickery 1984, Scott 1985). The absence of state provision did not necessarily equate with illegitimacy, since few expected the state to provide anyway; this sentiment finds contemporary expression in Afghanistan (Coburn 2009); Sierra Leone and Cambodia (Boas 2001, Roberts 2011); Liberia (Boas 2001); Nepal (Askvik et al. 2011) and a variety of other places. Failure to do in the past something that was not expected anyway did not mean 'states' or metropolitan power were delegitimated; just that they had performed in accordance with negative expectations, and that legitimacy had not been accorded them in the first place. Whilst no concept of a social contract, or of a neutral bureaucracy, or of impartial and legal rule existed to legitimate elites in the eyes of local populations, simultaneously the lack of reach and impact on many lives at various times made the state a non-event; a matter of inconsequence in daily routines; a set of organs disconnected from daily acts and outcomes.

This 'null' legitimacy finds expression in the postconflict scenario, as one might expect given the persistent character of the state in the parts of the world where peacebuilding happens, although the data is primarily anecdotal. A teacher at Kabul University made this point clear when s/he declared that 'ordinary people do not consider matters of legitimacy and whether [an] election process is transparent; the things that are most important for them are peace, security and jobs' (Coburn 2009, p. 3). Whether local or national government has a role in any of those may be secondary, since the private sector is active in security and jobs, and peace may be undermined by governmental activities anywhere. This is a useful illustration of null legitimacy, and the notion becomes evident when focus groups are asked about legitimacy during surveys. In such conditions, the concept of 'legitimacy' has often provoked confusion, discussion and dissent, frequently not translating easily in the first instance (Moe 2009, Roberts 2011). To many survey respondents, the idea of a state being anything other than authoritarian, corrupt and/or violent is antithetical to the collective experience of numerous colonial and post-colonial societies. Survey data from Southern Sudan (above) suggest that for many respondents in the harsh spaces characteristic of postconflict peacebuilding, having a 'liberal' government is not substantially different from any preceding metropolitan institutionalism. Many of the same faces are reshuffled, uniforms discarded or adopted, and the usual election promises made. All too often, as the literature increasingly suggests, little else changes, and there is no surprise that a corresponding lack of expectation of legitimacy or otherwise prevails. Discussions about state legitimacy with local people oftentimes provoke ribaldry rather than regard. The corruption that people associate with elite and indeed local power often delegitimizes the concept long before it is sustained or discredited.

The sense that any new postconflict government, which is normally composed of various combinations of the same characters who have been neglecting, abusing or co-opting the conflicted society, will behave any differently in the light of new nomenclature, is often not taken very seriously in postconflict spaces. In Freetown, Sierra Leone, for example, taxi drivers who work the town centre near an advertising billboard promoting the all-new 'anti-corruption' department of the government declare with conscious irony that it is the most corrupt department in the government, reflecting a wider social consensus echoed in civil society in the capital and beyond (Roberts 2011). In many senses, government is not something with which substantial majorities have or expect to have constructive relationships. The increasingly well-documented persistence of the informal, coexisting both constructively and destructively in parallel with formal Weberian, liberal institutionalism (Jackson 2005, Bratton 2007, Lund 2007), is further testament to the enduring irrelevance of moribund institutions and structures to so many postconflict lives. This frequently renders discussions of state legitimacy moot; an oxymoronic conversation out of context of social experience, expectation and delivery.

Conclusion

Liberal peacebuilding is an interrupter device that slews political momentum towards pluralism and representation with the objective of legitimating itself as a cosmopolitan process and the institutions it emphasizes as a means of achieving peaceful politics. It is no bad thing for this. But it could do better. Currently, it misses a crucial opportunity to perform better where it perhaps performs worst, in the arena of legitimacy. But it cannot do this without making good on its rhetoric of participation. Perhaps the most important intervention liberal peacebuilders can engineer is to make the process of building peace more genuinely democratic in the sense of engaging local people from peace negotiations through implementation, in order that a given peace matches that which is sought. This could overcome the data gap, wherein knowledge of peacebuilding is primarily an external affair. Instead, the peacebuilding process could be designed for local, national and international peacebuilders to capture legitimacy by relating provision and priorities back to social preferences, identified in democratic fashion through meaningful inclusivity. Data is not absent; it often resides in alternate silos of knowledge or can be mined with some degree of effort and the acceptance that no research can be perfect. The material gleaned from Southern Sudan shows that opinion on priorities is divided and that the idea of state legitimacy and illegitimacy is not of core concern to many people, who instead seek redress for disadvantage in local, informal institutions whilst ignoring, bypassing and circumventing formal liberal bodies if they offer little of relevance or utility—as Migdal *et al.* predicted (Migdal 1974, Migdal *et al.* 1994). It suggests strongly that an alternative epistemology is required to investigate how local determinism could be more of an influence in the earlier stages of designing and prioritizing peacebuilding institutions that could work in association with liberal interventionism and hegemony.

Notes on Contributor

David Roberts is Senior Lecturer in Peace and Conflict Studies at the University of Ulster.

References

Afoaku, G., 2005. *Explaining the failure of democracy in the Democratic Republic of Congo: autocracy and dissent in an ambivalent world*. Ceredigion: Edwin Mellen Press.

Afrobarometer, 2002. *Afrobarometer Briefing Paper No. 1*. Available from: http://www.afrobarometer.org/papers/AfrobriefNo1.pdf [Accessed 14 July 2010].

Amin, S., 1997. *Imperialism and unequal development: essays by Samir Amin*. Brighton: The Harvester Press.

Askvik, S., Jamil, I. and Dhakal, T.N., 2011. Citizens' trust in public and political institutions in Nepal. *International political science review*, 32 (4), 417–435.

Autesserre, S., 2010. *The trouble with the Congo: local violence and the failure of international peacebuilding*. Cambridge: Cambridge University Press.

Beckford, G., 1983. *Persistent poverty: underdevelopment in plantation economies of the Third World*. London: Zed.

Boas, M., 2001. Liberia and Sierra Leone—dead ringers? The logic of neopatrimonial rule. *Third world quarterly*, 22 (5), 697–723.

Bradbury, M., 2008. *Becoming Somaliland*. London: James Currey.

Brahimi, L., 2007. *Statebuilding in crisis and postconflict countries*. 7th Global Forum on Reinventing Government, Vienna. Available from: http://unpan1.un.org/intradoc/groups/public/documents/UN/UNPAN026305.pdf

Bratton, M., 2007. Formal versus informal institutions in Africa. *Journal of democracy*, 18 (3), 96–110.

Bulmer, M. and Warwick, D.P., 1993. *Social research in developing countries: surveys and censuses in the Third World*. London: Routledge.

Call, C., 2008. Building states to build peace? *In*: C. Call and V. Wyeth, eds. *Building states to build peace*. Boulder, CO: Lynne Rienner.

Cammack, D., 2007. The logic of African neopatrimonialism: what role for donors? *Development policy review*, 25 (5), 599–614.

Carothers, T., 2002. The end of the transition paradigm. *Journal of democracy*, 13 (1), 5–21.

Chabal, P., 2009. *Africa: the politics of suffering and smiling*. London: Zed.

Chandler, D., 1999. *Bosnia: faking democracy after Dayton*. London: Pluto.

Chandler, D., 2010a. *International statebuilding: the rise of post-liberal governance*. London: Routledge.

Chandler, D., 2010b. The uncritical critique of 'liberal' peace. *Review of international studies*, 36 (special issue), 137–156.

Chesterman, S., 2004. *You the people: the United Nations, transitional administration and state-building*. Oxford: Oxford University Press.

Coburn, N., 2009. *Some Afghan views on the government, the international community, and the 2009 elections*. Kabul: Afghanistan Research and Evaluation Unit.

Dahl, R., 1971. *Polyarchy: participation and opposition*. New Haven, CT: Yale University Press.

Desai, V. and Potter, R., 2006. *Doing development research*. London: Sage.

Devereux, S. and Hoddinott, J., 1993. *Fieldwork in developing countries*. Boulder, CO: Lynne Rienner.

Duffield, M., 2008. Global civil war: the non-insured, international containment and post-interventionary society. *Journal of refugee studies*, 21 (2), 145–165.

Egnell, R. and Halden, P., 2009. Laudable, ahistorical and overambitious: security sector reform meets state formation theory. *Conflict, security and development*, 9 (1), 27–54.

Eizenstat, S., Porter, E.J. and Weinstein, J., 2005. Rebuilding weak states. *Foreign affairs*, 84 (1), 134–146.

Englebert, P., 2002. *State legitimacy and development in Africa*. Boulder, CO: Lynne Rienner.

Fanthorpe, R., 2005. On the limits of liberal peace: chiefs and democratic decentralization in post-war Sierra Leone. *Africa affairs*, 105 (418), 27–49.

Francois, M. and Sud, I., 2006. Promoting stability and development in fragile and failed states. *Development policy review*, 24 (2), 141–160.

Fuller, A., 1992. Toward an emancipatory methodology for peace research. *Peace and change*, 17 (3), 286–311.

Gilley, B., 2009. *The right to rule: how states win and lose legitimacy*. New York: Columbia University Press.

Grindle, M., 2004. Good enough governance: poverty reduction and reform in developing countries. *Governance*, 17 (4), 525–548.

Heder, S., 1995. Cambodia's democratic transition to neoauthoritarianism. *Current history: a journal of contemporary world affairs* (December), 425–429.

Howella, J. and Linda, J., 2009. Manufacturing civil society and the limits of legitimacy: aid, security and civil society after 9/11 in Afghanistan. *European journal of development research*, 21 (5), 718–736.

Jackson, P., 2005. Chiefs, money and politicians: rebuilding local government in postwar Sierra Leone. *Public administration and development*, 25 (1), 49–58.

Jalali, A., 2006. The future of Afghanistan. *Parameters* (Spring), 4–19.

Jhazbhay, I., 2009. *Somaliland: an African struggle for nationhood and international recognition*. Johannesburg: Institute for Global Dialogue & South African Institute of International Affairs.

Kanharith, K., 1998. Phnom Penh, *Cambodia Daily*, 19 September.

Klugman, J. and Kallau, E.G., 2009. *Developmental transformation and peace consolidation in Southern Sudan*. Available from: http://www.fmreview.org/textOnlyContent/FMR/24/06.htm [Accessed 14 June 2011].

Krause, K. and Jutersonke, O., 2005. Peace, security and development in postconflict environments. *Security dialogue*, 36 (4), 447–462.

La Sage, A., 2002. Somalia: sovereign disguise for a Mogadishu mafia. *Review of African political economy*, 29 (91), 132–138.

Leca, J., 1990. Individualism and citizenship individualism. *In*: P. Birbaum and J. Leca, eds. *Individualism*. Oxford: Clarendon Press.

Ledwidge, F., 2011. *Losing small wars: British military failure in Iraq and Afghanistan*. New Haven, CT: Yale University Press.

Liden, K., Mac Ginty, R. and Richmond, O.P., 2009. Introduction: beyond northern epistemologies of peace: peacebuilding reconstructed? *International peacekeeping*, 16 (5), 587–598.

Little, E. and Logan, C., 2008. *The quality of democracy and governance in Africa: new results from Afrobarometer Round 4*. Available from: http://www.afrobarometer.org/papers/AfropaperNo108_21may09_newfinal.pdf [Accessed 14 July 2010].

Lizee, P., 2000. *Peace, power and resistance in Cambodia: global governance and the failure of international conflict resolution*. London: Macmillan.

Lund, C., 2007. *Twilight institutions: public authority and local politics in Africa*. Oxford: Blackwell Publishing.

Mac Ginty, R., 2010. Hybrid peace: the interaction between top-down and bottom-up peace. *Security dialogue*, 41 (4), 391–412.

McMillan, J., 2005. Promoting transparency in Angola. *Journal of democracy*, 16 (3), 155–169.

Migdal, J., 1974. *Peasants, politics and revolution: pressures toward political and social change in the third world*. Princeton, NJ: Princeton University Press.

Migdal, J., Kohli, A. and Shue, V., 1994. *State power and social forces: domination and transformation in the third world*. Cambridge: Cambridge University Press.

Mikkelsen, B., 2005. *Methods for development work and research: a guide for practitioners*. London: Sage.

Moe, L.W., 2009. *Negotiating political legitimacy: the case of state formation in post-conflict Somaliland*. Available from: http://cigj.anu.edu.au/cigj/link_documents/IssuesPapers/Wiuff.pdf.

O'Lear, S., 2007. Azerbaijan's resource wealth: political legitimacy and public opinion. *The geographical journal*, 173 (3), 207–223.

Ottaway, M., 2002. Rebuilding state institutions in collapsed states. *Development and change*, 33 (5), 1001–1023.

Paris, R., 2010. Saving liberal peacebuilding. *Review of international studies*, 36 (2), 337–365.

Peake, G. and Scheye, E., 2005. To arrest insecurity: time for a revised security sector reform agenda. *Conflict, security and development*, 5 (3), 295–327.

Pugh, M., 2002. Postwar political economy in Bosnia and Herzegovina: the spoils of peace. *Global governance*, 2, 467–482.

Rennie, R., Sharma, S. and Sen, P., 2008. *A survey of the Afghan people: Afghanistan in 2008*. Kabul and San Francisco: The Asia Foundation. Available from: http://asiafoundation.org/resources/pdfs/Afghanistanin2008.pdf

Richmond, O., 2008. *Peace in international relations*. London: Routledge.

Richmond, O., 2009a. A post-liberal peace: Eirenism and the everyday. *Review of international studies*, 35, 557–580.

Richmond, O., 2009b. Becoming liberal, unbecoming liberalism: liberal-local hybridity via the everyday as a response to the paradoxes of liberal peacebuilding. *Journal of intervention and statebuilding*, 3 (3), 324–344.

Roberts, D., 2001. *Political transition in Cambodia, 1991–1999: power, elitism and democracy*. London, NJ: Curzon.

Roberts, D., 2011. *Liberal peacebuilding and global governance: beyond the metropolis*. London: Routledge.

Sawyer, E., 2008. Remove or reform? A case for (restructuring) chiefdom governance in post-conflict Sierra Leone. *African affairs*, 107 (428), 387–403.

Schomerus, M. and Allen, T., 2010. *Southern Sudan at odds with itself: dynamics of conflict and predicaments of peace*. London: Development Studies Institute, LSE.

Scott, J.C., 1985. *Weapons of the weak: everyday forms of peasant resistance*. New Haven, CT: Yale University Press.

Sidahmed, A.S., 2010. Institutional reform and political party engagement: challenges to democratic transformation in post-CPA Sudan. *International journal of African renaissance studies—multi-, inter- and transdisciplinarity*, 5 (1), 19–35.

Snyder, R., 2000. Explaining transitions from neopatrimonial dictatorships. In: R. O'Kane, ed. *Revolution: critical concepts in political science*, Vol. IV. London: Routledge.

Sorensen, J.S., 2002. Balkanism and the new radical interventionism: a structural critique. *International peacekeeping*, 9 (1), 1–22.

Symons, J., 2010. The legitimation of international organisations: examining the identity of the communities that grant legitimacy. *Review of international studies*, 37 (5), 2557–2583.

Unsworth, S. and Moore, M., 2010. Societies, states and citizens. *Centre for the Future State*, 1–15. Available from: http://www.dfid.gov.uk/r4d/PDF/Outputs/FutureState/policymakers-guide.pdf.

Vickery, M., 1984. *Cambodia 1975–1982*. Boston, MA: Southend Press.

Weinstein, J., 2005. *Autonomous recovery and international intervention in comparative perspective*. Stanford, CA: Stanford University.

Williams, M., 2004. Leading from behind: democratic consolidation and the chieftaincy in South Africa. *The journal of modern African studies*, 42 (1), 113–136.

Wilson, J.Z., 2004. Paradoxes and dilemmas of institutional change: human rights and livelihoods in rural war-torn Angola. *Journal of peacebuilding and development*, 2 (1), 37–50.

Young, T., 1994. 'A project to be realised': global liberalism and contemporary Africa. *Millennium: journal of international studies*, 24 (3), 527–546.

Zakaria, F., 1997. The rise of illiberal democracy. *Foreign affairs*, (November/December), 22–43.

Everyday Legitimacy and International Administration: Global Governance and Local Legitimacy in Kosovo

Nicolas Lemay-Hébert

International administrations are a very specific form of statebuilding. This article examines the limits illustrated by the experience in Kosovo. Here, the international administration faced the same requirements of any legitimate, liberal government, but without the checks and balances normally associated with liberal governance. Thus, the international administration was granted full authority and the power thereby associated, but without the legitimacy upon which the liberal social contract rests. The statebuilding agenda put forth came to be seen as more exogenous, reinforcing the delegitimization process. This article specifically addresses the influence of the Weberian approach to legitimacy on the statebuilding literature, as well as its limits. It then proposes other possible avenues for statebuilding, more in line with a wider understanding of legitimacy and intervention.

Introduction: The Need to Reassess the International Involvement in Kosovo

The idea of direct governance by an outside organization of war-torn or 'dysfunctional' societies retains a pervasive influence in academia and some policy circles, despite the controversial experiences of places such as Kosovo and Timor-Leste. Most recently, and of direct concern to this special edition is the question of legitimacy and the evolving view that parachuting external, liberal values on their own into postconflict spaces may not be enough to allow for stable statebuilding of any kind. This article is concerned with the legitimacy gap that appears when the priorities and concerns of imported institutions are at odds with the priorities and needs of heterogeneous populations' everyday life.

This contribution builds on the previous literature on the subject, which has made considerable leeway in increasing the awareness of challenges that confronted the UN in the statebuilding process in Kosovo (Yannis 2001, 2004,

Chesterman 2004, Caplan 2005, Hehir 2006, 2007, 2009, King and Mason 2006, Narten 2008). Recognizing the contribution made by this literature, this article will provide additional layers of theorization. First, it will review the Weberian conceptions of statehood in the statebuilding literature, and its relationship to the concept of legitimacy. If the UN, as an international trustee, has successfully contributed to the institutional reconstruction of Kosovo, including the capacity to 'monopolize the legitimate use of physical force', it has also had difficulty nurturing and fostering local legitimacy in the daily governance of the territory. This 'legitimacy dilemma' happens despite the best intentions of international administrators, whose externally-mandated preferences tend to further delegitimate their intervention. Mirroring the state-strength dilemma identified by Kalevi Holsti (1996), this is a process that defies even well-intentioned officials. A second section analyses the 'legitimacy dilemma' and its implication in the delegitimization process that confronted international officials in the conduct of the mandate. In this section, the article takes a closer look at the rise of the Vetëvendosje! Movement as a force of contestation to local perceptions of the legitimacy of the international architecture put in place in 1999, and a third section will demonstrate that dynamics other than ethnic rivalries were at work in the events, notably the frustration over the delay in addressing the status question. Finally, the article will look briefly at the latest developments in the region, and other avenues for statebuilding in Kosovo.

Weber, Statehood and Statebuilding

The Weberian approach to statehood is the starting point for a number of analyses on state collapse and statebuilding. Weber (1948b, p. 78) famously defines the state 'as a human community that successfully claims the monopoly of the legitimate use of physical force within a given territory'. Following this definition, the state's ability to provide security is the benchmark according to which each state can be judged. Besides security, other criteria also have to be taken into account, all related to the capabilities of the state to secure its grip on society. The predominant approach involves the 'institutional approach' advanced notably by the likes of Gerald Helman, Steven Ratner, Francis Fukuyama and Robert Rotberg, among others, tend to focus on the administrative capability of the state and the ability of the state apparatus to affirm its authority over the society (Helman and Ratner 1992–93, Rotberg 2003, Fukuyama 2004). This institutionalist approach is central to the idea of transitional administrations, trusteeships and international administrations, as well as less disciplinarian interventions.

If (neo)Weberian approaches to statehood have profoundly influenced the statebuilding literature, the same could be said of the Weberian legacy regarding legitimacy. If Weber is rightly regarded as one of the most influential thinkers in social science, his contribution regarding the concept of legitimacy has been deemed highly controversial. For David Beetham (1991, p. 8), 'on the subject of legitimacy, his influence has been an almost unqualified disaster'. However, according to Beetham and others, the main mistake is not Weber's, but that of those social scientists who have reduced the explanation of beliefs to the processes and agencies of their dissemination and internalization (Beetham 1991, p. 10, Hobson and Seabrooke 2001). Nevertheless, Weber conceives legitimacy as a necessary condition and a means for a government to exercise authority over society. This could be done either by charismatic, traditional or rational–legal principles, to take up the three well-known ideal types presented by Weber (1947, p. 130). In that sense, legitimacy principles are in fact principles of legitimization of the central authority. For Weber, the claim of legitimacy is a bid for a justification of support, and its success consists not in fulfilling normative conditions but in being believed. He defines legitimacy as 'the prestige of being considered exemplary or binding' (Weber 1962, p. 72). To a certain extent, Weber's definition of legitimacy goes back to his own definition of politics: 'we wish to understand by politics only the leadership, or the influencing of the leadership, of a political association, hence today, of a state' (Weber 1948a, p. 77). Thus, it could be argued that Weber's conception of politics, and political legitimacy, is closely linked to his own conception of the state.

Weber's definition of legitimacy led Hanna Pitkin (1972, p. 281) to argue that it was 'essentially equivalent to defining "legitimate" as "the condition of being considered legitimate," and the corresponding "normative" definition comes out as "deserving to be considered legitimate"'. It is also on that ground that Peter Blau (1970, p. 149) states that Weber 'takes the existence of legitimate authority for granted and never systematically examine the structural conditions under which it emerges out of other forms of power,' while Carl Friedrich (Friedrich 1963, p. 186) posits that Weber's analysis 'assumes that any system of government is necessarily legitimate'.

Weber's conception of legitimacy has been quite influential, leading many social scientists in the twentieth century to follow the Weberian definition of legitimacy as *belief* in legitimacy. For instance, Seymour Lipset (1959, p. 86) defines legitimacy of a political system as its capacity 'to engender and maintain the belief that the existing political institutions are the most appropriate ones for the society'. Richard Merelman (1966, p. 548) considers legitimacy as 'a quality attributed to a regime by a population. That quality is the outcome of the government's capacity to engender legitimacy'. Charles Tilly (1985, p. 171) is also resolutely Weberian when he states that 'legitimacy depends rather little on abstract principle or assent of the governed. ... Legitimacy is the probability that other authorities will act to confirm the decisions of a given authority'. Accordingly, scholars following the institutional approach to statebuilding, under the influence of Weber's pioneering work, tend to treat legitimacy either as a mere consequence of functioning institutions or as a process of legitimization. This naturally stems from the Weberian approach of legitimacy. As Robert Grafstein (1981, p. 456) states, 'Weber virtually identifies legitimacy with stable and effective political power, reducing it to a routine submission to authority'.

Hence, we will analyse each aspect separately while addressing recent developments in the literature of statebuilding.

Robert Rotberg's work is certainly a good example of the tendency to reduce legitimacy to a consequence of 'stable and effective political power'. Mentioning legitimacy only as a consequence of good delivery of public goods, he argues that public goods 'give content to the social contract between ruler and ruled' (Rotberg 2004, pp. 2–3). He notes that 'there is no failed state without disharmonies between communities', but considers these 'disharmonies' as consequences of the failure of state institutions (Rotberg 2003, p. 4). Hence, legitimacy in that regard is treated as a natural by-product of successful state institutions. Once again, it all comes back to the definition of the state that one adopts. The author mentions that 'a nation-state also fails when it loses legitimacy, that is, when its nominal borders become irrelevant and autonomous control passes to groups within the national territory of the state, or sometimes even across its international borders' (Rotberg 2003, p. 9). The Weberian conception of the state cannot be more emphasized in that regard. The other tendency, 'reducing legitimacy to a routine submission to authority', is encompassed in Francis Fukuyama's work, for instance, with the specific emphasis the author puts on democracy as a legitimizing factor for the institutionalization process in a weak state. According to him, the only viable and durable source of legitimacy in today's world is liberal democracy (Fukuyama 1989, p. 3, 2004, p. 26).

Hence, one can argue that insisting on the political concept of legitimacy allows us to concentrate our attention on the state and society as distinct in terms of 'actors' though not necessarily autonomous institutions and activities. As Alexander Wendt (1999, p. 199) stated, 'it seems impossible to define the state apart from "society." States and societies seem to be conceptually interdependent in the same way that masters and slaves are, or teachers and students; the nature of each is a function of its relation to the other'. In that regard, it appears crucial to understand state and society in their mutually constitutive relationship, where legitimacy conditions state strength and is, at the same time, an element of state strength. As Beetham (1991, p. 11) states, 'a given power relationship is not legitimate because people believe in its legitimacy, but because it can be justified in terms of their beliefs'.

The overwhelming influence of the Weberian approach in the statebuilding literature will lead to a certain bias in international interventions, best summarized as the 'more is better' approach, where the more intrusive the intervention is, the more successful the outcome would be. The institutional focus will lead interveners to believe they can proceed with statebuilding activities without entering in the realm of nationbuilding (Lemay-Hébert 2009). Additionally, the mental conception the interveners have of a territory and its institutions will impact the actual intervention and the means used by the international community to address statebuilding challenges (Lemay-Hébert 2011). As it will be seen in the next sections, the approach used by the international community in Kosovo will carry in its own architecture the ferment of the delegitimation process.

Everyday Legitimacy and Legitimacy Dilemma in Kosovo

Following the NATO Operation Allied Force that expelled the Federal Republic of Yugoslavia's forces out of Kosovo, the United Nations Security Council passed Resolution 1244 of 10 June 1999. The resolution established an international civil and security presence to administer Kosovo, UNMIK and the NATO-led Kosovo Force respectively. The United Nations Interim Administration Mission in Kosovo (UNMIK)'s mandate as stipulated in Resolution 1244 was threefold: to establish a functioning interim civil administration, to promote the establishment of substantial autonomy and self-government, and finally to facilitate a political process to determine Kosovo's future status. One innovative feature of the mandate was the concentration of powers to the Special Representative of the Secretary-General (SRSG), who, as the legal head of state of Kosovo, enjoys 'virtually unlimited powers' (Mertus 2003, p. 28). He was given the responsibility to assure the coherence of the whole mission and to facilitate the political process designed to determine Kosovo's future status. Hence, not only was he empowered to assume full interim administrative responsibility over the territory of Kosovo, he was also given a central political role in settling the conflict. The civilian mandate was at first to 'oversee and, where necessary, conduct a number of civil affairs functions, such as the civil service and economic and budgetary affairs, as well as support the restoration and provision in the short run of basic public services, such as public health, education, utilities, transport and telecommunications'. However, the SRSG office subsequently extensively interpreted its own mandate. As Marcus Brand (2003, p. 9) recalled: '"basic civilian administrative functions" came to mean that *all* administrative functions (as basic as they may be under the given circumstances), are exercised by UNMIK alone'. The SRSG competencies would be defined by the Constitutional Framework for Provisional Self-Government in 2001. Despite the transfer of competencies in certain fields, the SRSG retained oversight of most competencies, which will lead to public clashes with local institutions.

Strictly speaking, there is no separation of powers in the framework of the international administration of Kosovo.

> [E]xecutive, legislative, and judicial authority are vested in a single individual (the transitional administrator), whose decisions cannot be challenged by the local population, whose actions are not always transparent, and who cannot be removed from power by the community in whose interests he or she exercises authority ostensibly. (Caplan 2005, p. 196)

In practice, not only is the SRSG not accountable to the local population, but he enjoys a certain degree of autonomy from the UN structure as well. Bernard

Kouchner, who acted as SRSG from July 1999 to January 2001, helped establish the autonomy of the position by reinforcing its own guard of political advisers and sidelining the UN's Department of Political Affairs (O'Neill 2002, p. 41). While the SRSG's potential role in the Kosovar political process was huge, the expectations of Kosovars were no less. The fact that UNMIK was 'exercising the sovereign prerogatives of a state' and 'functioning exactly like a government' (Blair 2002, pp. 10–40) had specific repercussions on the legitimacy of the intervention. Placed in the situation of a de facto government of Kosovo, the international administration had to face the same requirements that any legitimate government has. The international administration had the hard task to convince the local population of the legitimate character of its rule.

UNMIK's institutional legacy has been significant. The UN has notably succeeded in establishing a modicum of stability in the months following the 1999 war. It contributed to the creation of the Kosovo Police Service and the development of the justice system. Major violent crimes decreased throughout the first three years of the UN administration. In 1999, 245 people were murdered. By 2002, this number was reduced to 68. Over this same period, the rate of attempted murder dropped 48 per cent; kidnapping 44 per cent; attempted kidnapping 41 per cent; robbery 25 per cent; and arson 9 per cent (Jones et al. 2005, pp. 49–50). Furthermore, in the first two years, UNMIK had made substantial strides in creating a set of economic policy institutions in Kosovo. It was even considered the best managed of the US post-Cold War ventures in nationbuilding (Dobbins et al. 2003, p. 126).

However, the institutional output of the mission between 1999 and 2004 has not been sufficient to establish its credibility in the eyes of the population. One interesting feature in Kosovo is the presence of an Early Warning System, conducted by the United States Agency for International Development (USAID), the United Nations Development Programme (UNDP) and Riinvest, a local think tank. In that regard, one cannot help but notice the failure of UNMIK to secure popular legitimacy among Kosovars from all communities. From the highpoint of 63.8 per cent satisfaction with UNMIK's performance during the period of September–October 2002, UNMIK's ratings have steadily decreased to 20.7 per cent between January and April 2004 and now stand at 22.2 per cent according to the latest polls (UNDP and USAID 2010, p. 5). The results of the Early Warning System have been strengthened by the findings of a team of researchers from the Feinstein International Famine Center. Their research on the ground conducted in 2005 demonstrated that 'perceptions among the local population of UNMIK varied but were frequently damning. UNMIK was widely viewed as an arrogant bureaucracy, which was seen as feeding on itself' (Donini et al. 2005, p. 31). In fact, the most damning reviews of UNMIK came from international staff with experience in Kosovo. Lesley Abdela, OSCE deputy director for democratization-building in Kosovo, noted that 'by the time I left Kosovo in December 1999, UNMIK had squandered its honeymoon period ... By mid-October, it had become clear that the international community was fast losing credibility' (Abdela 2003, p. 209). Hansjörg Strohmeyer, who played a prominent role in UNMIK, recalls the progression of the Albanian sentiment in a simple sentence: 'just before the UN moved in, the Albanians were forced to give the three-finger Serb salute. When the UN arrived, they gave us the peace sign. And then after we'd been there a week, they gave us the middle finger' (Power 2008, p. 280). For Justice Goldstone, chair of the International Independent Inquiry on Kosovo, 'Kosovo is effectively under colonial rule. During my most recent visit to Kosovo, the distrust of the administrative and political capacity of the Albanian population was palpable' (Goldstone 2002, p. 145). Hence, if the international military campaign rode on a wave of popular sentiment (King and Mason 2006, p. 79), and if during the initial months of the intervention UNMIK was able to justify and legitimize its presence to a certain extent, with its honeymoon over, UNMIK had a hard time convincing the local population of the legitimate character of its rule and administration.

One central dynamic confronting international administrations is the legitimacy dilemma. Indeed, much of what international administrators do to reinforce their rule also perpetuates their weakness, a process which mirrors Kalevi Holsti's concern with the 'state-strength dilemma'. For Holsti (1996, p. 117), the weak state, 'in its attempt to find strength, adopts predatory and kleptocratic practices or plays upon and exacerbates social tensions between the myriads of communities that make up the society. Everything it does to become a strong state actually perpetuates its weakness'. And, like Holsti's state-strength dilemma, the legitimacy dilemma applies to international administrators and well-intentioned and honest leaders.

Albin Kurti's 'route of resistance' tells a lot about the legitimacy dilemma facing international administration. Probably the biggest non-violent resistance movement to the international administration in Kosovo, Vetëvendosje! started as a movement against the occupation of Serbia in Kosovo in 1997. The Kosovo Action Network (KAN), as it was known at this time, campaigned for clarifying the fate of missing persons in Kosovo and organized petitions and non-violent student protests. Albin Kurti, who was a student leader and one of the leaders of the movement, acquired national fame by being a political prisoner of Milošević's state. He was released in December 2000, and his fame was increased by the stark contrast it created with the image of the non-violent leader and future President of Kosovo, Ibrahim Rugova, shaking hands with Milosević on 15 May 1999.

However, after 1999, the movement started to be marginalized in Kosovo and was looking for a new direction. Quickly enough, the movement turned to oppose the 'anti-democratic regime of UNMIK'. The movement officially changed in 2004. In what was considered the conceptual genesis of the movement, a 'Citizen's Declaration' was read in front of UNMIK buildings and precisely on the fifth anniversary of the Resolution 1244, and a promise was made to struggle against the illegitimate regime of UNMIK. For Kurti, UNMIK and Serbia are two sides of the same coin and one aspect of domination cannot be distinguished from the other.[1] One is external (Serbia), the other is internal (UNMIK), but they closely resemble each other. For him, the problem was not a couple of rotten apples in the barrel, but was systemic proportionate to the authority wielded by internationals. 'Absolute power isolates from power', Kurti added, loosely quoting from Hannah Arendt.[2]

Albin Kurti was arrested on 10 February 2007 after he led a demonstration against Maarti Ahtisaaris proposals (Special Envoy of the Secretary-General) for the final status of Kosovo, which he considers as a plan to retain a hold over the territory. The charges included 'participating in a crowd committing a criminal offence', and 'participating in a group obstructing official persons [police]'—although no other participant in the demonstration was so charged. He was also indicted for 'calling [people] to resistance'; again, no other member of the organizing group has been similarly charged. Furthermore, Kurti's arrest was condemned by a number of international NGOs, notably Amnesty International which called it a 'politically-motivated prosecution' (Amnesty International 2007). Howard Clark (2008), director of the pacifist movement War Resisters International concurs, stating that 'the prosecution of Albin Kurti is a politically motivated attempt to harass and discredit one of the most outspoken and persistent critics of the international administration of Kosovo and the movement Vetëvendosje (Self-Determination) which he helped found'. For Clark (2008), UNMIK 'has shown itself to be unaccountable and—in the face of pluralism and civil disobedience—quite simply authoritarian, failing to respect legal process'.

The International Helsinki Federation (IHF) which has been monitoring Kurti's trial, raised concerns concerning the independence of the judiciary, denouncing the fact that the international judge had approached the prosecutor after the hearing—in the absence of either Albin Kurti or his court-appointed lawyer—to clarify what the prosecution would like to recommend in relation to his detention (Chadbourne 2007). Julie Chadbourne of the Norwegian Helsinki Committee also stated that 'there are indications that [this case] is not up and up. There are questions that Kurti is being brought forward as a scapegoat' (Brownell 2007, Norwegian Helsinki Committee 2008). Furthermore, the IHF was refused access to Albin Kurti while in pre-trial detention by Kosovo Ministry of Justice officials on the grounds that he was a 'Category A' detainee, held exclusively under the jurisdiction of UNMIK. Amnesty International did not receive an answer from UNMIK when the organization asked for a legal definition of 'Category A' (Amnesty International 2007). As reported by Krenar Gashi (2007), Kosovo editor of the *Balkan Investigative Reporting Network*, 'while many in Kosovo may disagree with Kurti's actions, most people believe that he is being held isolated to prevent him from carrying on with his political activities while the status issue awaits its resolution'. In opposition to the whole process, six lawyers have refused to represent Albin Kurti during the trial, including Ramë Gashi, President of the Bar Association, who stated that he would not appoint another lawyer for the case (Amnesty International 2009). In 2010, Kurti was finally found guilty of obstructing official persons, while other charges of participating in a crowd committing criminal acts and inciting violence were dropped. Kurti was immediately released for time already served.

In effect, it is hard to precisely assess the support enjoyed by the Vetëvendosje! movement in the Kosovar-Albanian community. The attendance at political rallies conducted by the self-determination movement has been generally low, the biggest crowd being at the February 2007 demonstration, which attracted 2,000 to 3,000 demonstrators. The movement claims to have a network of 10,000 followers, among its 16 branches in Kosovo (Karpat 2006). However, apart from the direct involvement in the movement's actions, a more general sense of the support for the movement can be found by a careful study of the Early Warning Reports. The Early Warning System has included questions regarding Vetëvendosje!'s support in the Kosovar-Albanian community from the fourteenth edition (July–September 2006) until the seventeenth edition (April–June 2007). However, quite interestingly, these questions, after being included in the annexes of the fourteenth edition, were placed in the 'public and personal security' chapter rather than the political chapter in the fifteenth to seventeenth editions. Moreover, the overall support was not assessed, only the support by region or by education. It is hard to derive any consistent information from these figures, given the shaky nature of demography statistics in Kosovo. Moreover, quite tellingly, until the January–March 2007 edition, the reports included a quite tendentious question concerning the relationship between the feeling of security and the support expressed to Vetëvendosje!. The Early Warning System removed altogether references to Vetëvendosje! after the April–June 2007 edition, the last time the support for the student movement was assessed. However, the fourteenth edition provides an idea of the overall support expressed to the student movement, with 64.4 per cent of the Kosovar-Albanian respondents supporting the movement 'to a certain extent' or more. The results of the movement in the latest 2010 national elections, which finished third with a surprising 12.2 per cent of the vote, is a clear indication that the movement is not a marginal force in Kosovo. If anything, his conviction earlier this year for obstructing officials in the 2007 Pristina protests 'has strengthened its popularity' (Collaku 2010).

March Events: Extent of the Discontent in Kosovo

If the year 2004 saw the birth of a bona fide movement of contestation to UNMIK's rule, it was also the year of the largest violent incident since the 1999 Kosovo War. It took a dramatic event, the March 2004 riots, where Serbian communities and cultural sites were attacked, to make UN officials realize the extent of the political discontent in Kosovo. It has to be recalled that 2004 was the low-point of popular satisfaction with UNMIK management of Kosovo and all indicators showed alarming trends for the UN. As noted by the Early Warning System team,

> optimistic assessments of international and domestic actors regarding the progress achieved and the absence of security threats did not correspond with

the indicators that showed an increase of the dissatisfaction of Kosovo citizens. Previous public opinion polls, carried out within the EWS project have anticipated aggravating trends in many areas that indicated the possibility of destabilization. (UNDP, USAID and Riinvest 2004, pp. 1–2)

Among the worrying trends, the authors noted that support for UNMIK and the SRSG has been plunging: 'During the period November 2002–March 2004, satisfaction with the performance of UNMIK and the SRSG decreased by about 40%, satisfaction for the Assembly decreased by about 10% and for the Government of Kosovo by some 5%' (UNDP, USAID and Riinvest 2004, pp. 1–2).

The common explanation was nevertheless that the same old divisions were at work and UNMIK was just a spectator in this disaster. *The Independent* ran the following headline on 19 March 2004: 'Kosovo has been a model of nation-building, we cannot now allow it to disintegrate', while Gabriel Partos of the BBC referred to 'the worst inter-ethnic clash in four years' without mentioning acts against the UN on 17 March 2004. On 19 March *The Guardian* also blamed 'the deep and intense hatred between 2 million ethnic Albanians and fewer than 100,000 Serbs'. However partially true, this simplistic explanation brushes aside other aspects of these events.

In the midst of the events, 19 persons died and 954 were injured (United Nations 2004, para. 3). Many Serb houses and churches were burnt, leaving irreparable damage to relations between the two communities. The events are generally believed to have been triggered by the death of three Albanian children by drowning in the Ibar River near the Serb community of Zubin Potok. The story spread by word of mouth that the children were chased by Serbs before their death, which sparked Albanian attacks on Serb enclaves. Though the circumstances of that incident have not been established clearly, the incident precipitated spontaneous Albanian demonstrations.[3] The demonstrations were quickly taken over by 'organized elements', and intense fighting erupted between the two communities while the violence quickly spread to other cities. UNMIK estimates that 51,000 people were involved in 33 riots. The March violence forced out the entire Serb population from dozens of locations and affected Roma and Ashkali communities.

For the majority of observers, the events indicated that long-standing grievances on all sides were ready to erupt into violence. However, another point is generally overshadowed, which is that the reactions between the Serb and Albanian community reflected deep frustrations with the international administration. As Nexhmedin Spahiu (2004, p. 124), political analyst and Director of Radio and TV Mitrovica, asserts:

the fact that violence in Kosova is being considered as interethnic violence by the international media and the United Nations Security Council is just a result of successful disguise of the real problems of Kosova by UNMIK. ... the attacks of Kosova Albanians against Serbs are a result of the conflict between the majority population in Kosova and UNMIK.

Though there was clearly an inter-ethnic aspect of the violence that erupted in 2004, it cannot be disputed that UNMIK was targeted by Albanian mobs. As King and Mason recalled, Albanian mobs during the events 'turned their collective fury on their international overlords, throwing rocks at UN buildings, burning UN flags and destroying more than 100 of the administration's ubiquitous white Toyota 4Runner 4x4s' (King and Mason 2006, p. 6). Hence, during the events, 'Kosovo's international institutions—including UNMIK and KFOR—were themselves under attack and needed protection, drawing resources away from protection of minorities' (Human Rights Watch 2004, p. 26). A UN high-level report leaked to the press even mentioned that 'many [of international officials interviewed] believe that UNMIK and Kosovo Force (KFOR) would have collapsed had the riots gone on for another day or two. The mission was already on the point of overstaying its welcome' (Jennings 2004).

Moreover, there were prior signs of tensions between the international community and the Albanian extremists. Faton Klinaku, head of the 'war associations',[4] told a crowd in Pristina on 16 March: 'the neo-colonialists called UNMIK are supporting organized crime and are continuing the same politics applied by Serbia' (Human Rights Watch 2004, p. 18). Some violent incidents were recorded in Prizren, where a group of demonstrators stoned UNMIK regional headquarters. Also, a homemade explosive device containing five kilos of TNT was planted near UNMIK headquarters just ahead of a visit by Jean-Marie Guehenno, Under-Secretary-General for Peacekeeping Operations, on 6 March 2004. According to Ben Lovelock (2005, p. 146), this event 'turned out to be a harbinger of what was to come'.

In a rare show of unity, the majority of the citizens of Kosovo in a July 2004 poll, regardless of their respective community (Serb, Albanian or 'other'), placed responsibility for the situation and crisis in March 2004 within UNMIK: 73.5 per cent of Kosovar Albanians, 58.4 per cent of Kosovar Serbs and 58.3 per cent of other minority groups advanced this opinion (UNDP, USAID and Riinvest 2004, p. 6). This is probably the most troubling aspect of the March events for the international administration. Despite NATO's KFOR mandate to provide hard security, that organization managed to avoid blame in the public eye for the international failure to provide local security so evident in March 2004. In fact, NATO approval ratings have steadily hovered around 80 per cent, even during the March crisis, making it one of the most respected political entities in Kosovo. Hence, if, for Kosovars of all communities, 'the main responsibility lies with KFOR and UNMIK, as they have to guarantee freedom and security for all the citizens of Kosovo', as the editorial team from *Koha Ditore* put it in 2004, it seems that only UNMIK paid the price in terms of popular perception.

Of course, the Provisional Institutions of Self Government (PISG) has its share of blame for the events, as the local media and the critics against UNMIK most certainly exaggerated, as claimed by Deputy International Administrator Charles Brayshaw, but this is to a certain extent beside the point. What is important here is to understand how UNMIK came to be perceived as the actor bearing the responsibility for the crisis and political situation, while the PISG and KFOR managed to avoid most of the blame. This goes back directly to the legitimacy dilemma and the limits of Weberian approaches to statebuilding. While some commentators claim that the issue was that there were not enough troops in Kosovo to assure the protection of minorities (Murphy 2007, p. 197), other elements seem important to understand in order to avoid similar events in the future. For Krenar Gashi, Kosovo editor of the Balkan Investigative Reporting Network (BIRN), UNMIK's ratings have been falling and led to violent confrontations not because 'people hate internationals, but because they hate absolute control', hence echoing unconsciously the remarks of Albin Kurti reported earlier and the legitimacy dilemma.[5] In the context of direct governance, UNMIK has been unable to generate sufficient legitimacy to justify its rule over the territory, setting the stage for being targeted as an exogenous presence. In that regard, Veton Surroi predicted more violence if there is no change in the way the international community runs the territory: 'the international community woke up in March, but I don't think it's out of bed yet'.

The SRSG Bernard Kouchner, in his farewell speech in 2001, urged his successor, Hans Haekkerup, to share responsibility with the local population or risk the backlash inevitable in any colonial rule. 'I tell him not to lose your time in setting up a better administration', said Kouchner, 'help them here to set one up. Don't play the game of an eternal mandate.' If the political situation in Kosovo following 1999 required an international presence, other statebuilding avenues were possible back then. In order to provide an alternative to direct governance by UNMIK, the Independent International Commission on Kosovo proposed in 2001 what it called 'conditional independence', which is 'quite distinct from limited self-rule under UNMIK'. The proposal was to allow Kosovo to control the whole range of powers reserved to the SRSG, but under conditions that would ensure stability in the region: explicit renunciation of any changes of borders, a constitutional guarantee of human rights for all citizens, the renunciation of violence in settling internal or external disputes, and a commitment to regional cooperation (Independent International Commission on Kosovo 2001, pp. 25–27). The Commission noted that 'if the population is distrusted, it is likely to repay like with like' (International Commission on Kosovo 2001, p. 21). For Kreilkamp (2002, p. 652), 'it suggests that there are potential alternatives to the hard-line approach that has been adopted by the Security Council' in the first years of the intervention.

According to an internal UNMIK document, one of the lessons learned from the experience of the UN administration of Kosovo is that 'the Mission demonstrated a lack of cultural sensitivity and an insufficient understanding of the dynamics of the society, in terms both of power structures and of negotiations'. Hence, 'cultural sensitivity and understanding of local society must be the guiding principles for policy planning and implementation' for future civil administration missions. Certainly, cultural sensitivity, along with robust accountability mechanisms and a greater local ownership of the process, can help the mission garner a certain degree of legitimacy. However, as David Harland (2004, p. 15) notes, 'all international administration, however benign, is to some extent illegitimate.

International administration, even when it is aligned with the wishes of the people concerned, is almost always imposed from outside'.

It is not yet clear whether Kosovo and Timor-Leste should be regarded as 'historic anomalies' (Willner-Reid 2005–6, p. 6), representing a 'high-water mark of UN peace operations' (Chesterman 2004, p. 97) or features of the international life 'likely to remain with us for some time' (Mortimer 2004, p. 12). What is certain is that in Kosovo, the progressive handover of supervision competencies to the European Union and to the International Civilian Office (ICO) gave the chance for internationals to reflect on the international experiment so far. Torbjorn Sohlstrom, Head of International Civilian Office Preparation Team, stated in 2007 that the new international presence 'will have a very different relationship with the authorities of Kosovo'. He further emphasized that 'the international community will no longer seek to govern Kosovo. People often suggest that the ICO will be the successor of UNMIK. That is not the intention' (Sohlstrom 2007, p. 50). For the former President of Kosovo, Kosovars stands ready to welcome a light international civilian presence, 'as long as Kosovo does not have to face another UNMIK in the next phase' (Sejdiu 2007, pp. 47–48). For Blerim Shala (2007, p. 55), Coordinator of Kosovo Negotiation Team's working groups, 'experience so far shows us the path that we need not follow'. One must wonder if this fictional independence will be sufficiently attractive to persuade those Kosovar-Albanian militants to accept a prolonged period of administration. For Veton Surroi (2007, pp. 51–52), the civilian presence 'can be called easy, mild, good, but still the international community will have an intervention capacity'. The Kosovar are preoccupied with the ICO's right of interpretation as to what is within its mandate. The most 'confusing' element in the Ahtisaari document 'is the "spirit of the document" which serves as a light post, giving the ICR wide discretionary powers not only to interpret the terms of the document, but also to model all the legislation of Kosovo in line with the spirit' (KIPRED 2007, p. 7). In that regard, there is a very tangible risk that Kosovo takes the Bosnian route, a parallel reinforced notably by an EU official, Caspar Klynge, when mentioning that 'the plan is to provide the EU with a similar authority as the Senior High Representative in Bosnia and Herzegovina, so that it could intervene politically by annulling decisions and replacing officials who were in breach of laws' (NATO Parliamentary Assembly 2006, para. 20).

Conclusion

The main argument of this contribution is that statebuilding should not be understood simply as institutional reconstruction. The neo-Weberian logics of statebuilding can place interveners in a difficult situation when the time comes to legitimate the international agenda. The setup of an international administration with executive, legislative and judicial powers put the international officials in an intractable conundrum, resulting in a 'legitimacy dilemma': what the interveners do to reinforce their legitimacy perpetuates their weakness. The state-building agenda comes to be seen as progressively more exogenous, further reinforcing the delegitimization process. It is important to reinforce the argument that it is a structural dynamic, not only related to a few 'bad apples in the barrel', as stressed by some opponents to the international administration. In that regard, the Western-oriented conception of state, state legitimacy and statebuilding can incite resistance, 'reflecting the common emergence of a local post-colonial narrative about liberal peacebuilding's endorsement of an international–local relationship, configured as managers and subjects' (Richmond 2009, p. 558).

This configuration of allegiances, prioritizing the interests and politics of the international community to the detriment of the context, needs and interests of local constituents, has had clear repercussions for the constitution of the social order in Kosovo, and continues to have even today (Visoka and Bolton 2011). Indeed, according to Jitske Hoogenboom (2011, p. 5), 'over the past 12 years, authorities in Kosovo have been primarily accountable to the international community, instead of their own community. Up until today, international actors have had a mandate to overrule decisions of the Kosovo Government, or at least to influence them substantially, often from behind the scenes'. This has led to a very unbalanced process of liberal statebuilding, where international officials were placed in a position of full authority, at least until March 2004, but without benefiting from the legitimacy upon which the liberal social contract rests. As this article argued, it is a process that is consistent with neo-Weberian conceptions of state and legitimacy which constitute the orthodoxy in the field today. The Weberian conception of the state—emphasizing the administrative capability of the state and the ability of the state apparatus to affirm its authority over the society—and the Weberian definition of legitimacy as *belief* in legitimacy have had a profound impact on current statebuilding approaches and practices, neo-Weberians deriving from Weber's work a model of international intervention, where 'more is better'. However, on the everyday level, the international administration in Kosovo was deeply problematic, unable as it was to be seen as a legitimate authority by its local subjects, all communities included. The Kosovo experiment stands as a useful reminder that the institutional focus, so pervasive in the contemporary literature on statebuilding, leaves crucial elements out of the equation, such as the structural conditions under which legitimacy emerges in statebuilding processes, conditions which should be explored and not taken from granted in the context of international interventions.

Acknowledgements

My thanks go to Robert Bailey, Danielle Beswick, Paul Jackson, Stefanie Kappler, Heather Marquette, David Roberts and two anonymous reviewers for their comments on previous versions of this article. This work was supported by project PEACE—'Local Ownership and Peace Missions', financed by the Marie Curie Actions (FP7).

Notes on Contributor

Dr. **Nicolas Lemay-Hébert** is a Marie Curie Experienced Researcher in the International Development Department of the University of Birmingham, UK.

Notes

1 Interview with Albin Kurti, Head of the Movement Vetevendosje!, 15 July 2007, Pristina, Kosovo.
2 For instance, Hannah Arendt (1973) exposes in *The origins of totalitarianism* how power became the essence of political action and the center of political thought when it was separated from the political community which it should serve.
3 A UN official claimed that the violence was planned, saying that 'nothing in Kosovo happens spontaneously' (Robinson 2004). However, there is no actual proof that these events were planned prior to March 2004. Solana's analysis seems more accurate: 'it may have been a moment of spontaneity, but ... a lot of people [were] organized to take advantage of that moment of spontaneity' (Ames 2004).
4 The 'war associations' include KLA's war veterans, KLA invalids and the families of the missing.
5 Interview with Krenar Gashi, Kosovo editor of BIRN, 10 July 2007, Pristina.

References

Abdela, L., 2003. Kosovo: missed opportunities, lessons for the future. *Development in practice*, 13 (2–3), 208–216.
Ames, P., 2004. EU's Solana says violence could delay decision on Kosovo's future. *Associated press*, 25 March.
Amnesty International, 2007. Document—Serbia (Kosovo): Albin Kurti—a politically motivated prosecution, 10 December. Available from: http://www.amnesty.org/en/library/asset/EUR70/014/2007/en/fa20afdc-a73a-11dc-9249-5f9f850000d6/eur700142007eng.html
Amnesty International, 2009. *Amnesty International report: Serbia*. Available from: http://thereport.amnesty.org/en/regions/europe-central-asia/serbia.
Arendt, H., 1973. *The origins of totalitarianism*. New York: Harvest.
Beetham, D., 1991. *The legitimation of power*. Basingstoke: MacMillan.
Blair, S., 2002. *Weaving the strands of the rope*. Halifax, NS: Centre for Foreign Policy Studies.
Blau, P., 1970. Critical remarks on Weber's theory of authority. *In*: D. Wrong, ed. *Max Weber*. Englewood Cliffs, NJ: Prentice-Hall.
Brand, M., 2003. *The development of Kosovo institutions and the transition of authority from UNMIK to local self-government*. Geneva: CASIN report.

Brownell, G., 2007. The blue jailers. *Newsweek*, 10 December.

Caplan, R., 2005. *International governance of war-torn territories*. Oxford: Oxford University Press.

Chadbourne, J., 2007. The Kurti case: law or politics? *Koha Ditore*, 15 May.

Chesterman, S., 2004. *You, the people: the United Nations, transitional administration, and state-building*. Oxford: Oxford University Press.

Clark, H., 2008. Kosovo: international pacifist organisation calls for end of prosecution of Albin Kurti. Statement of *War Resisters' International*, 1 February. Available from: http://www.wri-irg.org/statemnt/kurti08-en.htm.

Collaku, P., 2010. Albin Kurti, guardian of flame of Kosovo nationalism. *Balkan insight*, 8 December.

Dobbins, J. et al., 2003. *America's role in nation-building: from Germany to Iraq*. Santa Monica, CA: RAND.

Donini, A. et al., 2005. *Mapping the security environment: understanding the perceptions of local communities, peace support operations, and assistance agencies*. A Feinstein International Famine Center Report Commissioned by the United Kingdom NGO–Military Contact Group.

Friedrich, C., 1963. *Man and his government: an empirical theory of politics*. New York: McGray-Hill.

Fukuyama, F., 1989. The end of history? *The national interest*, 16, 3–18.

Fukuyama, F., 2004. *State-building: governance and world order in the 21st century*. Ithaca, NY: Cornell University Press.

Gashi, K., 2007. Kurti case presents legal headache for UN in Kosovo. *Balkan investigative reporting network*, 2 October. Available from: http://www.birn.eu.com/en/106/10/5119/.

Goldstone, R., 2002. Whither Kosovo? Whither democracy? *Global governance*, 8 (2), 143–147.

Grafstein, R., 1981. The failure of Weber's conception of legitimacy: its causes and implications. *Journal of politics*, 43, 456–472.

Harland, D., 2004. Legitimacy and effectiveness in international administration. *Global governance*, 10 (1), 15–19.

Hehir, A., 2006. Autonomous province building: identification theory and the failure of UNMIK. *International peacekeeping*, 13 (2), 200–214.

Hehir, A., 2007. Determining Kosovo's final status: the viability of ongoing administration. *Civil wars*, 9 (3), 243–261.

Hehir, A., 2009. Intervention and statebuilding in Kosovo. *Journal of intervention and statebuilding*, 3 (2), 135–142.

Helman, G. and Ratner, S., 1992–93. Saving failed states. *Foreign policy*, 89, 1–20.

Hobson, J. and Seabrooke, L., 2001. Reimagining Weber: constructing international society and the social balance of power. *European journal of international relations*, 7 (2), 239–274.

Holsti, K., 1996. *The state, war, and the state of war*. Cambridge: Cambridge University Press.

Hoogenboom, J., 2011. The EU as a peacebuilder in Kosovo. Paper presented at the CSDN Meeting in Bucharest, 28 June.

Human Rights Watch, 2004. Failure to protect: anti-minority violence in Kosovo, March 2004. *Human rights watch*, 16 (6), 1–66.

Independent International Commission on Kosovo, 2001. *The follow-up of the Kosovo Report: why conditional independence?* Stockholm: Global Reporting Books.

Jennings, C., 2004. NATO peacekeepers 'unable' to keep lid on violence in Kosovo. *The Scotsman*, 2 September.

Jones, S. et al., 2005. *Establishing law and order after conflict*. Santa Monica, CA: RAND.

Karpat, C., 2006. Albin Kurti: the youthful symbol of non-violence. *AIA Balkanian Section*, 24 January. Available from: http://www.axisglobe.com/article.asp?article=618.

King, I. and Mason, W., 2006. *Peace at any price*. New York: Cornell University Press.

KIPRED, 2007. *Analysis of the comprehensive package for the status of Kosovo*. Pristina: Kosovo Institute for Policy Research and Development (KIPRED).

Kreilkamp, J., 2002. UN postconflict reconstruction. *New York University journal of international law and politics*, 35 (3), 619–670.

Lemay-Hébert, N., 2009. Statebuilding without nationbuilding? Legitimacy, state failure and the limits of the institutionalist approach. *Journal of intervention and statebuilding*, 3 (1), 21–45.

Lemay-Hébert, N., 2011. The 'empty-shell' approach: the setup process of international administrations in Timor-Leste and Kosovo, its consequences and lessons. *International studies perspectives*, 12 (2), 190–211.

Lipset, S., 1959. Some social requisites of democracy. *American political science review*, 53 (1), 69–105.

Lovelock, B., 2005. Securing a viable peace: defeating militant extremists—fourth-generation peace implementation. In: J. Covey, M. Dziedzic and L. Hawley, eds. *The quest for viable peace: international intervention and strategies for conflict transformation*. Washington, DC: United States Institute of Peace.

Merelman, R., 1966. Learning and legitimacy. *American political science review*, 60, 548–561.

Mertus, J., 2003. The impact of intervention on local human rights culture: a Kosovo case study. *The global review of ethnopolitics*, 1 (2), 21–36.

Mortimer, E., 2004. International administration of war-torn societies. *Global governance*, 10 (1), 7–14.

Murphy, R., 2007. *UN peacekeeping in Lebanon, Somalia and Kosovo*. Cambridge: Cambridge University Press.

Narten, J., 2008. Dilemmas of promoting local ownership: the case of postwar Kosovo. In: R. Paris and T. Sisk, eds. *The dilemmas of statebuilding: confronting the contradictions of postwar peace operations*. London: Routledge.

NATO Parliamentary Assembly, 2006. Visit to Vienna and Kosovo by the sub-committee on NATO partnerships, 4–6 October.

Norwegian Helsinki Committee, 2008. The Kurti case: fair trial? 31 January.

O'Neill, W., 2002. *Kosovo: an unfinished peace*. London: Lynne Rienner.

Pitkin, H., 1972. *Wittgenstein and justice*. Berkeley, CA: University of California Press.

Power, S., 2008. *Chasing the flame*. New York: Penguin Press.

Richmond, O., 2009. A post-liberal peace: Eirenism and the everyday. *Review of international studies*, 35, 557–580.

Robinson, M., 2004. Kosovo clashes were planned, says UN official. *The Scotsman*, 18 March.

Rotberg, R., 2003. Failed states, collapsed states, weak states: causes and indicators. In: R. Rotberg, ed. *State failure and state weakness in a time of terror*. Washington, DC: Brookings Institution Press.

Rotberg, R., 2004. The failure and collapse of nation-states. In: R. Rotberg, ed. *When states fail: causes and consequences*. Princeton, NJ: Princeton University Press.

Sejdiu, F., 2007. Address. In: Riinvest and Soros Foundation, eds. *Post-status status: international oversight in Kosovo*. Pristina: Forum 2015.

Shala, B., 2007. Address. In: Riinvest and Soros Foundation, eds. *Post-status status: international oversight in Kosovo*. Pristina: Forum 2015.

Sohlstrom, T., 2007. Address. In: Riinvest and Soros Foundation, eds. *Post-status status: international oversight in kosovo*. Pristina: Forum 2015.

Spahiu, N., 2004. Dhunë ndëretnike apo revoltë ndaj UNMIK-tu? [Inter-ethnic violence or revolt against UNMIK?]. *In*: N. Spahiu, ed. *Drej Kombit Kosovar*. Mitrovicë: Biblioteka Kombëtare dhe Universitare e Kosovës.

Surroi, V., 2007. Address. *In*: Riinvest and Soros Foundation, eds. *Post-status status: international oversight in kosovo*. Pristina: Forum 2015.

Tilly, C., 1985. War making and state making as organized crime. *In*: P. Evans, D. Rueschemeyer and T. Skocpol, eds. *Bringing the state back in*. Cambridge: Cambridge University Press.

United Nations, 2004. *Report of the Secretary-General on the United Nations Interim Administration Mission in Kosovo*, UN. Doc. S/2004/348, 30 April.

UNDP and USAID, 2010. *Public Pulse Report 1*. Available from: http://www.kosovo.undp.org/repository/docs/public-pulsenglish-web.pdf.

UNDP, USAID and Riinvest, 2004. *Early Warning Report 7*. Available from: http://www.ks.undp.org/repository/docs/ewr_7engl.pdf.

Visoka, G. and Bolton, G., 2011. The complex nature and Implications of International engagement after Kosovo's independence. *Civil wars*, 13 (2), 189–214.

Weber, M., 1947. *The theory of social and economic organization*. London: William Hodge.

Weber, M., 1948a. Class, status and party. *In*: H. Gerth and C.W. Mills, eds. *From Max Weber: essays in sociology*. New York: Oxford University Press.

Weber, M., 1948b. Politics as a vocation. *In*: H. Gerth and C.W. Mills, eds. *From Max Weber: essays in sociology*. New York: Oxford University Press.

Weber, M., 1962. *Basic concepts in sociology*. New York: Citadel Press.

Wendt, A., 1999. *Social theory of international politics*. Cambridge: Cambridge University Press.

Willner-Reid, M., 2005–6. Post-colonial governments of leading strings. Unpublished paper presented at Coimbra University.

Yannis, A., 2001. Kosovo under international administration. *Survival*, 43 (2), 31–48.

Yannis, A., 2004. The UN as government in Kosovo. *Global governance*, 10 (1), 67–81.

Index

Note: Page numbers in **bold** type refer to figures
Page numbers in *italic* type refer to tables
Page numbers followed by 'n' refer to notes

Abdela, L. 92
Afghanistan government 34
African states survey 72-3
Afrobarometer 72-3
Albanians 93, 96-7
alien nation 1
Allen, T.: and Schomerus, M. 67, 80
Alter Art 20, 22, 23
Amin, S. 81
Amnesty International 94
arena: cultural 12, 19-25; semi-public 7, 18-25
Arendt, H. 12-13, 101n
art festivals 21-3

Banja Luka (BiH): Museum for Contemporary Arts 22; Protok 21
Barakat, S.: *et al* 60
Basic Packages of Health Services (BPHS) 33-4
Beetham, D. 89, 90
Bellina, S.: *et al* 5
Berlin, I. 66
Berman, B. 16
Bjune, G.: and Gele, A.A. 31
Blau, P. 89
Bosnia-Herzegovina (BiH) 11-28; art festivals 21-3; Centre for Interdisciplinary Research of Visual Culture 19-20; constitutional arrangement 14; constitutional reform 17; cultural actors 20-1; cultural arenas 12, 19-25; distrust in politicians 17-18; ethnic identities 14; European Union (EU) 14-15, 17; everyday experiences 12, 23-5; everyday problems 18; frustrations 18; hydro-electric facilities 15; international community 17-18; Office of the High Representative (OHR) 14, 15, 16-18; ownership 22; political elites 14-15, 16; political situation 11-12, 21; polls 11-12; public sphere 14-15, 24; semi-public arena 18-25; social life 19; state system 14-15, 16; theatres 19, 21; unhappy people 11-12
Boutros-Ghali, B. 15
Brand, M. 91
Brayshaw, C. 97
Buden, B. 18-19

Call, C. 2-3
Cambodia 71
Canavan, A.: *et al* 32
Capplan, R. 91
Carothers, T. 67
castes 50
ceremonies 56
Chabal, P. 69
Chadbourne, J. 94
Chandler, D. 15, 17, 66, 67, 69
Chesterman, S. 99
Cichon, M.: and Hagemejer, K. 6
Clapham, C. 6
Clark, H. 94
Clark, I. 16
Coburn, N. 82
Coleman, K. 15
Collaku, P. 95
Colombo, A.: and Pavignani, E. 31
Colvin, C.J. 58
Commission for Welcome, Truth and Reconciliation (Timor-Leste 2005) 49, 52, 54, 56, 58-60
Communist Party of Nepal (Maoist, CPN-M) 50

community: international 17-18
Community Reconciliation Process (CRP) 49, 58
Comprehensive Peace Agreement (CPA, Sudan 2005) 76
conflict 34-5, 37-8; impact on health programmes 30-1
Cornwall, A. 19
countries: infrastructure 74; poor 75
Cramer, C.: and Goodhand, J. 29
cultural arenas: Bosnia-Herzegovina (BiH) 12, 19-25

Dahl, R. 67
Darcy, J.: and Pavanello, S. 35
Dayton Peace Agreement (DPA 1995) 14
democracy 67, 73, **78**; electoral 4; legitimacy 4; liberal 1; mature 6
Department for International Development (DFID) 36
discourse: legitimacy 81; rights 45, 48; statebuilding 35
distributed peace 59
Divjak, B.: and Pugh, M. 15
Donais, T. 15
Donini, A.: et al 92
Duffield, M. 70
Duplex Gallery (Sarajevo, BiH) 23

Early Warning System: Kosovo 92, 95; UNDP Report (2010) 11
economic development 36
Eizenstat, S.: et al 71-2
Eldon, J.: et al 32, 35, 36, 38
electoral democracy 4
elites: political 14-15, 16
ethnic identities 14
European Union (EU) 14-15, 17
Evans, M.: et al 60
everyday 67-8; life 7, 12, 18, 23-5; needs 47, 60-1

families, needs 51, 52-5, *53*
Fanthorpe, R. 74
Fatimie, A. 34
Foucalt, M. 13
Fox, J. 12
Francois, M.: and Sud, I. 4, 47, 71
Freidrich, C. 89
Fritz, V.: and Menocal, A.R. 35
Frljić, O. 21

Gashi, K. 94, 98, 101n
Gashi, R. 94
Geertz, C. 51

Gele, A.A.: and Bjune, G. 31
global governance: Kosovo 4, 87-104
global legitimacy 69-70
Goldstone, R. 93
Goodhand, J.: and Cramer, C. 29
Gordon, S. 7, 29-44; et al 36
governance: global 4, 87-104; good 46; local 4; postconflict 45
government: Afghanistan 34; Mozambique 31; South Sudan 76
government legitimacy 3, 46-8; good governance 46
Grafstein, R. 89
Grindle, M. 4-5, 71, 72, 75
Gusmão, X. 49

Hadi, Y.: et al 32, 35, 36, 38
Hagemejer, K.: and Cichon, M. 6
Harding, A.: and Loevinsohn, B. 33
Harland, D. 98-9
Hattori, R.: et al 56
Hayner, P. 45
health interventions: third party 29-44
health programmes 7; Basic Packages of Health Services (BPHS) 33-4; conflict impact 30-1; disruption 30-1; distortions 32; donors 33; economic development 36; examples 36; importance 38; literature 29-30, 35; population vulnerability 31; purpose 29; service delivery 35; stabilization 29-30, 38; strengthening 32-5; systems 30-8; targeting health workers 31; tool 29; tuberculosis (TB) 31
Heder, S. 67
Hohe, T.: and Nixon, R. 50
Holsti, K. 88, 93
Hoogenboom, J. 100
Horwitz, M. 14
Human Rights Watch 97
humanitarian programmes *see* health programmes

identities: ethnic 14
Independent International Commission on Kosovo (2001) 98
indigenous tradition 56-9
Innes, C.: and Lee, K. 37
Institute of Development Studies (IDS) 72
International Civilian Office (ICO) 99
International Committee of Red Cross (ICRC) 51, 61n
international community 17-18
International Helsinki Federation (IHF) 94
International Peace Institute (IPI) report (2011) 3

INDEX

International Security Assistance Force (ISAF) 36
interventions: liberal 65
invited spaces 19, 22

Jutersonke, O.: and Krause, K. 66

Kabil, N. 20
Kallau, E.G.: and Klugman, J. 76
Kanharith, K. 70
Kappler, S. 7, 8, 11-28
King, I.: and Mason, W. 97
Klinaku, F. 97
Klugman, J.: and Kallau, E.G. 76
Klynge, C. 99
Kosovo Action Network (KAN) 93
Kosovo Force (KFOR) 97
Kosovo Independent International Commission (2001) 98
Kosovo (international involvement) 91-100; demonstrations 95, 96; discontent 95-9; Early Warning System 92, 95; movement 95; statebuilding 87-104
Kouchner, B. 91-2, 98
Krause, K.: and Jutersonke, O. 66; and Milliken, J. 6, 46-7
Kreilkamp, J. 98
Krug, E.: *et al* 34
Kurti, A. 93-4, 101n

La'o Hamutuk 49
Lawoti, M. 59
Leca, J. 68, 71
Lee, K.: and Innes, C. 37
legitimacy 1-10; authority 59; concept 3; creation 4, 16; definition 89; discourses 81; empirical studies 47; gap 3; object 4; performance 4, 47, 60, 71; postconflict 46-7, 58-9; social construction 16
Lemay-Hébert, N. 8, 87-104
liberal democracy 1
liberal interventions 65
liberal orthodoxy 67, 68
Liberal Project 67
liberal states 70
liberalism 2, 9
Lindberg, S. 2
Lipset, S. 89
Little, E.: and Logan, C. 73
Lizee, P. 67
local governance 4
local legitimacy 2-3, 5, 7, 18, 68, 69-70; Kosovo 87-104
Loevinsohn, B.: and Harding, A. 33
Logan, C.: and Little, E. 73

London School of Economics (LSE) report (2010) 67, 77, 80

Madlingozi, T. 48
Maoists 50, 55
Mason, W.: and King, I. 97
Menocal, A.R.: and Fritz, V. 35
Merleman, R. 89
Mertus, J. 91
Miall, H.: *et al* 61
Millennium Development Goals (MDGs) 32-3
Milliken, J.: and Krause, K. 6, 46-7
missing people 51, 53, 61n
Moore, M.: and Unsworth, S. 65-6, 72
Mozambican government 31
Museum for Contemporary Arts (Banja Luka) 22

National Democratic Institute (NDI) 11, 76
NATO (North Atlantic Treaty Organization) 91, 97, 99
needs: everyday 47, 60-1; families 51, 52-5, *53*; people's 5-7, 25
Nepal 49, 50-1, 60-1; castes 50; Communist Party 50; feudal social relations 50; GDP 61n; geography 50; population 50; poverty 50; transition 50-1, *see also* victims' needs (Timor Leste and Nepal)
Nikolić, M. 21
Nixon, R.: and Hohe, T. 50
non-governmental organizations (NGOs) 32, 33

Ogura, K. 50
Omladinski Kulturni Centar (OKC) 21, 22, 23
Opération des Nations Unies au Congo (ONUC) 36
orthodox peacebuilding 5, 66
orthodoxy: liberal 67, 68
Ottaway, M. 67

Palmer, N.: *et al* 34; and Strong, L. 30
Papagianni, K. 5
Paris, R. 7
Partners Achieving Change Together (PACT) 80
Partos, G. 96
Pavanello, S.: and Darcy, J. 35
Pavignani, E.: and Colombo, A. 31
peace: distributed 59
peacebuilding: critical 2; orthodox 5, 66; policy 70; postconflict 1-3, 66; public priorities 79-80, **79**
peoples' needs 5-7, 25, *see also* victims' needs

Pilav, A. 21
Pitkin, H. 89
political elites 14-15, 16
Pontanima choir 20
populations: postconflict 47
Porter, J.E., et al 71-2
postconflict governance 45
postconflict legitimacy 46-7, 58-9
postconflict peacebuilding 1-2, 66; contemporary 66; prevailing approach 2-3
postconflict populations 47
postconflict societies 45
postconflict stabilization 2
postconflict victims *see* victims' needs (Timor Leste and Nepal)
poverty 50
Power, S. 93
private *vs* public sphere 13
Protok (Banja Luka) 21
Provisional Institutions of Self Government (PISG) 97
public order 5
public priorities 79-80, **79**
public realm 12-13
public space 12-18
public sphere 14-15, 24; *vs* private sphere 13
Pugh, M. 14; and Divjak, B. 15

Ramsbotham, O.: et al 61
regional legitimacy 17-18
Richmond, O. 59, 66, 67-8, 100
rights discourse 45, 48
Riinvest 92, 95-6
Roberts, D. 1-10, 65-86
Robins, S. 7-8, 45-64
Robinson, M. 101n
Romita, P.: et al 3
Rotberg, R. 90
Rothmann, I.: et al 32
Rothstein, B. 4
Rubinstein, L. 33, 34-5, 37

Sarajevo: Center for Contemporary Art (SCCA) 22; Duplex Gallery 23
Sarajlić-Maglić, D. 16, 18
Sawyer, E. 73-4
Schomerus, M.: and Allen, T. 67, 80
Schwarz, R. 12
security problem 1
Security Sector Reform (SSR) 5, 70-1
Sejdiu, F. 99
semi-public arena 7, 18-25
Serbs 93, 96-7
Šestić, B. 22
Sierra Leone 73-4, 82

Simmons, A.J. 46
Simonsen, S. 14
Slotin, J.: et al 3
societies: maldeveloped 74; postconflict 45
Sohlstrom, T. 99
Sondorp, E. 34, 39n
Sorensen, J. 67
Spahić, S. 19
Spahiu, N. 96
Special Representative of the Secretary-General (SRSG) 91-2, 96, 98
stability 1, 5, 6, 29, 32
stabilization: postconflict 2
statebuilding 5, 18, 29-30, 35-6, 38-9, 68, 87; discourses 34, 35; Kosovo 89-104; Weberian 67, 88-91, 98
statehood 89-90
states: failed 1; fragile 5, 35; liberal 70
Strohmeyer, H. 92-3
Strong, L.: and Palmer, N. 30
Sud, I.: and Francois, M. 4, 47, 71
Sudan: Comprehensive Peace Agreement (CPA 2005) 76
Sudan (South) survey 76-80, 82; government 76; results 77-80
Surroi, V. 99
survivors 61n

Teitel, R.G. 45
theatres 19, 21; international festival 19, 21
Tilly, C. 89
Timor-Leste 49-50, 60-1; Commission for Welcome, Truth and Reconciliation (2005) 49, 52, 54, 56, 58-60; GDP 61n; geography 49-50; leadership 49; population 50; poverty 50; violent past 49-50, *see also* victims' needs (Timor Leste and Nepal)
tradition: indigenous 56-9
Travnik (BiH): Centre for Culture 20
truth commission 49, 52, 54, 56, 58-60
tuberculosis (TB) 31

Uhlin, A. 16
United Nations (UN) 49, 70-1, 88, 91-2, 96, 101n; Security Council 91
United Nations Development Programme (UNDP) 92, 95-6; Early Warning System Report (2010) 11
United Nations Interim Administration Mission in Kosovo (UNMIK) 91-8
United States Agency for International Development (USAID) 37, 92, 95-6
Unsworth, S.: and Moore, M. 65-6, 72

Vergeer, P.: et al 32

INDEX

Veterans' Commissions 56
victims 52; approaches 48; re label as survivors 61n
victims' needs (Timor Leste and Nepal) 45-64; ceremonies 56; data 53, 56; everyday lives 47, 60-1; expressed 53, *53*; families 51; indigenous tradition 56-9; interviews 51; methodology 51; missing people 51, 53, 61n; sample 51; spirits 57; truth commission 49, 52, 54, 56, 58-60

Waddington, C.: *et al* 32, 35, 36, 38
Waldman, R. 37
war associations 101n
Weber, M. 59, 88-90
Weberian statebuilding 67, 88-91, 98
Weinstein, J.: *et al* 71-2

Weintraub, J. 13
welfare 6
Wendt, A. 90
Western policies 65
Wilder, A. 29
Willner-Reid, M. 99
Wilson, R.A. 46
Woodhouse, T.: *et al* 61
Woodward, S. 7
World Bank 17, 33, 61n
Wyeth, V.: *et al* 3

Young, T. 67

Zakaria, F. 67
Zwi, A. 31
Zyck, S.A.: *et al* 60